Teen
Dream Power

Teen Dream Power

Unlock the Meaning of Your Dreams

M. J. Abadie

Bindu Books
Rochester, Vermont

Bindu Books
One Park Street
Rochester, Vermont 05767
www.InnerTraditions.com

Bindu Books is a division of Inner Traditions International

Library of Congress Cataloging-in-Publication Data

Abadie, M. J. (Marie-Jeanne)
   Teen dream power : unlock the meaning of your dreams / M. J. Abadie.
      p. cm.
Contents: What dreams can do for you — Dream explorers around the world — Interpretation of dreams — Dreams and everyday life — Dream recall — Keeping a dream diary — Creating your personal dream diction-ary — Different states of dreaming — Dreams and spiritual development.
   ISBN 0-89281-086-6
 1. Teenagers' dreams. 2. Dream interpretation. 3. Symbolism (Psychology) 4. Teenagers' dreams—Problems, exercises, etc. [1. Dreams. 2. Dream interpretation.] I. Title.

   BF1099.T43 2003
   154.6'3'0835—dc21

                                                              2003004488

Printed and bound in United States at Lake Book Manufacturing, Inc.

10 9 8 7 6 5 4 3 2 1

Text design and layout by Mary Anne Hurhula
This book was typeset in Veljovic with Blackfriar as the display typeface

Contents

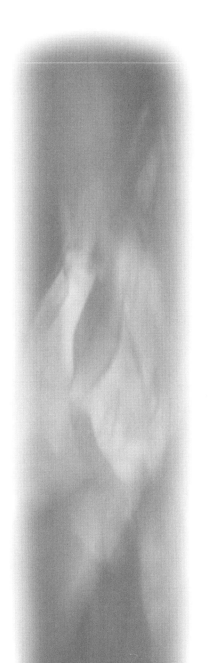

Acknowledgments

My thanks are extended to all those who have shared their dreams with me over the years, both clients and friends. From them I learned so much about the multileveled and fascinating world of others' dreams, which served to enhance my own personal dreaming experiences.

I owe a particular debt of gratitude to my longtime dreamwork partner, Mark Hasselriis, whose untimely death in 1999 deprived me of the major pillar of my most intensive years of dreamwork.

Also deserving of acknowledgment are those writers who have written about dreams and shared their precious knowledge with the world. I have been educated and inspired by many of them.

Closer to home, my thanks go to my always wonderful editor, Laura Schlivek, for her unfailing support and attention to the many tedious details involved in the journey of a manuscript into final form as a book.

To those others—publisher Ehud Sperling, acquisitions editor Jon Graham, managing editor Jeanie Levitan, designer Mary Anne Hurhula—on the staff of Inner Traditions, I offer my profound appreciation for their enthusiasm, care, and encouragement.

My thanks go to my dear friend Walter Allen for a timely suggestion that I investigate the connection between dreams and weather, which proved fruitful and added another dimension to my understanding of the nature of dreams.

Considering the nature of this book, it also seems appropriate to thank the dreaming process itself—whatever its true origins may be—without which there would be no book!

Preface

Dreams:
Your Hidden Resource

The world of dreams is many layered, infinitely rich and varied, stocked with the most astonishing possibilities: in it you can fly, move forward or backward in time, meet the living and the dead, experience total strangers, visit foreign countries, take a trip to outer space. The list is endless. On top of that, you can use your dreamtime to solve problems, receive information from mysterious sources—including your own unconscious mind—be creative, get ideas for new projects and ongoing activities. Most important, you can get in tune with your own inner psychological processes, which are constantly changing, as you yourself are constantly changing. All in all, dreaming is one of the most fascinating and rewarding activities available to human beings. Best of all, it's entirely *free* (and also nonfattening). However, let me issue a word of caution: dreaming can become addictive! So intriguing is this world inside you that comes vividly alive when you sleep that you may just want to spend a lot of time there. And that's okay. In fact, it's a good thing—as you will learn all through this book.

Now, you may be asking, *Why would someone write a book on dreams just for teens?*

The answer is both simple and complex. The simple part is this: as a teen you have the special opportunity to take advantage of your dreams while you are still in the process of becoming an adult. This is especially useful because you're in a time of rapid change and development. Your entire bodily chemical composition is changing—new hormones are being produced, your brain is generating its secret

Why Pay Attention to Dreams?

"Dreams are a reservoir of knowledge and experience, yet they are often overlooked as a vehicle for exploring reality."
Tibetan teacher Tarthang Tulku,
Openness Mind

"Our conscious minds are needed if we are to make the most of our dreams; by bringing them into waking consciousness and learning to understand them we may be led to a reappraisal of our whole mode of being."
Ann Faraday,
Dream Power

"When you look into yourself, the very effort involved extends the limitations of your consciousness, expands it, and allows you to use abilities that often you do not realize you possess."
Jane Roberts,
The Seth Material

substances that allow you to think and make mental connections, your emotions are in flux (sometimes swinging wildly around in the course of a few minutes). It's an exciting time, but not necessarily an easy one. Dreams can be of great help. Not only can you use your dreams to solve practical, everyday problems, you can get in touch with your inner self on a nightly (or daily) basis.

Did I say simple? Well, that *was* the simple part! So what's the complex part? The complex part is invisible. It's what is going on inside you all the time, the part you don't know about. While you sleep and dream, your inner mind is busy as a bee (and your body's chemical factory is also active producing dozens of substances that affect your growth, your brain, your emotions, and everything else about you). This deep mind is called the *unconscious*, and it never sleeps. Entire books have been written about the unconscious mind and its activities and processes, and more than a few books have been written about dreams and their connection to the unconscious mind. However, when all is said and done, dreaming remains a mystery. *That's the complex part!* The truth is that nobody, but nobody, really knows why we dream, where dreams originate, exactly what they mean, or much else about this most complex of human characteristics.

What we do know is that *everybody* dreams—even those who claim they don't. (They just don't remember their dreams.) If you tell a dream to someone, no matter how fantastic it sounds, you will be believed. No one will ever say, "Oh, you couldn't have dreamed *that*." Arguments may spring up about just about everything else (and teens spend a lot of time rapping about the questions about life to which there are no simple answers). But you'll never be accused of lying about dreaming.

The trick then is not that you have to *believe* in dreams. They are a fact of life, everyone's life. What you need to do is to *use* your dreams. Teaching you how to do that is the purpose of this special dream book for teens. By learning what dreams can do for you at this early and crucial stage of your life, you will have an advantage that will last you the rest of your life. Paying attention to your dreams is like putting money in the bank that will draw interest as you get older. When you sleep and dream, your unconscious mind is sending you important messages that may hold keys to your personal happiness, now and in the future.

This summary doesn't begin to cover all the dream possibilities, for that inner territory we visit each night (and during daytime naps, too) is extremely vast and mostly unexplored. But as you read through this book and do the exercises, you'll get an overview of what awaits you each time you catch a few ZZZZs.

The famous Swiss psychologist Carl Gustav Jung wrote, "The dream is a little hidden door in the innermost and most secret recesses of the soul, opening into that cosmic night which was psyche long before there was any ego-consciousness, and which will remain psyche no matter how far our ego-consciousness may extend. . . . In dreams we put on the likeness of that more universal, truer, more eternal [person] dwelling in the darkness of the primordial night."

Introduction
Wake Up to a World of Meaning

The famous English poet Samuel Taylor Coleridge posed this question:

> What if you slept, and what if in your sleep you dreamed, and what if in your dream you went to heaven and there plucked a strange and beautiful flower, and what if when you awoke you had the flower in your hand? Ah, what then?

We have all awakened from a particularly vivid dream with the gauzy sensation that it was *real,* that the experience was something that actually happened, and then—floating slowly up from the compelling world of dream into the facts of ordinary everyday reality—we wondered what it all meant.

Unfortunately, too many of us forget our dreams immediately upon awakening, if we have remembered them even for a moment. There's just always so much to *do* when morning arrives and we wake up to a new day. In the bustle of our daytime activities, we fail to pay attention to that wonderful, mysterious world of meaning that is revealed to us in our dreams. And this is a great loss. A Jewish proverb says, "An unremembered dream is like an unopened letter from God."

And yet, sometimes we find ourselves with the residue of a dream clinging to us, like dew on the grass before the sun has burned it off. It might be a misty feeling, like a fog through which we can see only dimly—yet it persists, asking for our attention. Most of us brush it away, like a bothersome fly settling on our bare skin, annoyed to be distracted from the task at hand, such as studying, planning an

"The future belongs to people who believe in the beauty of their dreams."
Eleanor Roosevelt, Former First Lady and U.N. Ambassador

1

The Uses of Dreams

Most dream researchers—and active dreamers from all walks of life—agree that we can all use our dreams as tools for understanding ourselves better, for dealing with and solving the problems of everyday life, and for gaining valuable information about our inner lives. As Carlos Casteneda, famed for his contact with a Native American shaman teacher, says in his book *The Art of Dreaming*, "Dreaming liberates perception, enlarging the scope of what can be perceived."

"We are such stuff
As dreams are made on, and our little life
Is rounded with a sleep."
William Shakespeare,
The Tempest

"I was not looking for my dreams to interpret my life, but rather for my life to interpret my dreams."
Susan Sontag,
The Benefactor

outing, or getting ready for school. Even so, some of the dream imagery will pop into consciousness when we are least expecting it, like a trick jack-in-the-box, a reminder from the unconscious that something important is happening within that requires our attention.

Suppose that instead of the above scenario of forgetting a dream and ignoring the flashes of it that occur during the day, you have taken the time to write down your dream and think about what it meant. Suddenly, things are very different! Now, you have captured your dream on paper and are free to interpret it, play around with its meaning, whatever you like—at your leisure. You've just taken a giant step into your own personal world of dream meanings. Doesn't that sound like a good idea?

Remember, you can use your dreams for a multitude of purposes, from psychological insight to sheer entertainment. In fact, you can use your dreams to help you handle all phases of your life, both inner and outer. This is especially important during your teen years when you are growing and developing in all areas: your body is changing rapidly, your mind is expanding into new horizons, your sexual nature becomes active, even urgent. And you are under increasing pressure from many sources—school, sports, activities, parental concerns, social life, sexual decisions. On top of it all, your spiritual life and your emotional fluctuations may cause considerable turmoil.

As you read through this book and do the exercises, you will discover how to learn to use time you may consider wasted. Believe it or not, lots of people (many active teens among them) consider sleep a big waste of valuable time they could spend "doing things." These unenlightened people really hate to spend their time sleeping because they think sleep is a zero and nothing worthwhile is happening. They couldn't be more wrong, as you will see. Sleeping does more than refresh and renew you for another busy day: your sleeping hours are prime time for you to commune with yourself at the deepest, most significant level.

Dreams weave the events of the day into a new pattern; they can even combine with previous dreams into a sort of recombinant dream chemistry. In this mysterious process, we are introduced to new levels of meaning in our lives, shown new ways of doing things, of thinking and perceiving. We are blessed by our visits to the strange inner territory of our personal dream world. Mythologist and philosopher Joseph Campbell, in his book *The Mythic Image,* comments thus:

> For in dreams, things are not as single, simple, and separate as they seem, the logic of Aristotle fails, and what is not-A may indeed be A. . . . [In] this one life-enclosing sphere of space-time, all things are brought to manifestation, multiplied, and in the end return to the universal womb that is night.

When you take an active interest in your dreams and learn to interpret them, it's like having a psychic savings account that builds your inner resources. And the more attention you pay to your dreams, by thinking about them and recording them, the more you will gain from your dream life. You will dream more, remember more, understand more. Your dreams will speak more clearly to you. You can have a relationship with your dream world that is just as real and valid as the one you have with your waking world.

And what an exciting relationship it can be! In chapter 1, you'll learn just what dreams can do for you, while chapter 2 will introduce you to the Dream Explorers of other cultures (for native and indigenous peoples have always held dreams to be important and sacred). Then, in chapter 3 you'll begin to learn the art of dream interpretation. You'll read some examples of real dreams others have had and what they meant, which will guide you into interpreting your own dreams.

Chapter 4 will show you how to access your dreams for specific purposes and how to get the most out of your dreamtime. Chapter 5 will teach you how to better recall your dreams—a valuable skill you'll use your whole life long. Following recall methods and tips, in chapter 6 you'll learn to keep a dream diary.

Moving along, chapter 7 will show you how to build your own dream dictionary of meanings. Chapter 8 will discuss different states of dreaming: those intriguing out-of-body experiences we hear about,

Take Naps!

No kidding—naps are excellent times for dreams. Any time of the day or evening that you can sneak in a nap is potential dreamtime. Not only that, but the dreams from different times of day, evening, night, and early morning, possess distinctly different qualities. You can have a lot of fun investigating this phenomenon.

"The mind doesn't just wander around in sleep without a purpose. It wants to bring back shapes and angles, golden ratios, oceans, and mountains—it wants to make order out of chaos. It seems to be this: It wants to dream up stories."

Popie Mohring,
Master Gardener

"I have never lost the sense that where my dreams come from is where I come from. And for that reason, they deserve serious study."

Elizabeth Rose, Editor
The Rose Reader

lucid dreaming (the art of *knowing* you are dreaming while you are still asleep and dreaming), and the bogeymen of dreams—nightmares—and what to do about them.

Finally, chapter 9 will talk about using your dreams for spiritual purposes, to reach higher states of consciousness.

A fascinating trip awaits you as you embark on this journey of self-discovery and sail into your own hidden sea of dreams. Enjoy it, learn from it, treasure it. It's a fabulous experience!

Dream Control

You can learn to "program" your dreams and acquire an extra dimension in your dream life that will help you grow into a mature adult. And you'll then have permanent access to the magical power of your dreams. Learning this technique will be of special aid to you at the critical time of life that your teen years are. With practice, you can learn to program your dreams to serve your needs, to let you get a handle on whatever needs handling.

Dream Time: Timeless Dreams

It has been estimated that the average person spends four or five *years* of a lifetime dreaming, but that figure is quite probably low. According to sleep lab studies, we dream on average one and a half hours during a normal eight-hour night's sleep. However, teens need more sleep than adults (though they often don't get the sleep they need because of overbusy schedules) and may well get in more dreamtime when they play "catch-up" on lost sleep during vacations and on weekends and holidays.

It doesn't matter how much actual time you spend dreaming: what you want is quality, not quantity. In addition, I suspect that the amount of dreaming varies with individual dreamers, and yours may increase as your interest in the dream process and interaction with it grow. Knowing the richness and variety of dreams, I always find it sad when people aren't interested in their own dreams. It's like not being interested in their own life with its many variations—emotions, love, spirituality. Ignoring dreams is like not knowing or caring about art, poetry, music. Truly, those who find sleep and dreams a waste of time are indeed wasting time. What is more, they are throwing away a precious resource.

Don't make that mistake! Start now to pay attention to your dreams and make it a habit. You won't regret it.

1

What Dreams Can Do for You

Your dream world is an invisible but extremely powerful inner resouce, one that you can learn to access freely. You can learn to command and control your dreams, thereby enriching your life immeasurably.

Once upon a time not so long ago, an inventor was struggling with a major problem. His name was Elias Howe, and for years he had been trying to solve this problem, so that he could complete a machine he was building—a machine that would in time change the world. He was missing a small but vital detail, and, try as he would, he just couldn't figure it out. Needless to say, Howe was a very frustrated man. One night, after another long day of fruitless work on his project, he dreamed he had been captured by fierce savages. These warriors were attacking him with spears. Although in the dream he was terrified he would be killed, he noticed that the spears were unusual looking: each one had an eye-shaped hole at the pointed end. When Howe woke up, it hit him like a brick: he had actually *dreamed* the answer to his problem. His nightmare was a blessing in disguise. He immediately saw that the eye of the spear could be an eye in a sewing needle, near its point. Elated with the discovery, he rushed to his laboratory and finished the design of his invention: the sewing machine. The rest, as they say, is history.

The list of what dreams can do for you seems endless. We've touched on a few of these benefits of dreaming in the preface and introduction. Now let's go into a bit more detail. I want you to get really excited about your own dream potential. And, once you realize the possibilities, I think you will.

5

FAMOUS DREAMERS

The history of dreams is filled with stories of famous people who have called on their dreams for help, or who have received help unexpectedly from their dreams. Here are a few more interesting stories to illustrate the point:

The physicist Niels Bohr, who developed the theory of the movements of electrons, had a dream in which he saw the planets attached to the sun by strings. This image inspired him to finalize his theory.

The great Albert Einstein reported that the famous theory of relativity came to him while he was napping—a good reason for taking frequent naps!

Author Richard Bach, who wrote the bestseller *Jonathan Livingston Seagull,* was stuck in a writer's block after writing the first half of his now-famous novel. It was eight years later that he literally dreamed the second half and was able to complete his book.

Swedish filmmaker Ingmar Bergman told reporters that his classic film *Cries and Whispers* had been inspired by a dream.

Another writer, the well-loved British author Robert Louis Stevenson, was quite dependent on his dreams for ideas that he could turn into sellable stories. Stevenson has related in his memoirs that after a childhood tortured by nightmares, and his successful efforts to overcome them, he was able to put his dreams to work for profit.

A born storyteller (though he started out as a medical student), he was accustomed to lull himself to sleep by making up stories to amuse himself. Eventually, he turned this personal hobby into a profession, becoming a writer of tales like *Treasure Island*. He identified his dream-helpers as "little people," or "Brownies." Once he was in constant contact with this inner source, his nightmares vanished, never to return. Instead, whenever he was in need of income he turned to his dreams:

> At once the little people begin to bestir themselves in the same quest, and labour all night long, and all night long set before him truncheons of tales upon their lighted theatre.

No fear of his being frightened now; the flying heart and the frozen scalp are things bygone; applause, growing applause, growing interest, growing exultation in his own cleverness . . . and at last a jubilant leap to wakefulness, with the cry, "I have it, that'll do!"

Stevenson wrote his autobiography in the third person, not revealing that he was the subject until the end.

Stevenson further states that sometimes when he examined the story his Brownies had provided, he was disappointed, finding it unmarketable. However, he also reported that the Brownies "did him honest service and gave him better tales than he could fashion for himself," that "they can tell him a story piece by piece, like a serial, and keep him all the while in ignorance of where they aim."

Stevenson's Brownies are a perfect example of dream helpers just waiting to be called upon. A particularly famous example of the work of Stevenson's Brownies is the tale *The Strange Case of Dr. Jekyll and Mr. Hyde.* As he explains:

I had long been trying to write a story on this subject, to find a body, a vehicle, for that strong sense of man's double being, which must at times come in upon and overwhelm the mind of every thinking creature. [After he destroyed an earlier version of the manuscript . . .] For two days I went about racking my brains for a plot of any sort; and on the second night I dreamed the scene at the window, and a scene afterwards split in two, in which Hyde, pursued for some crime, took the powder and underwent the change in the presence of his pursuers. All the rest was made awake, and consciously, although I think I can trace in much of it the manner of my Brownies.

Although Stevenson did the "mechanical work, which is about the worst of it," writing out the tales with pen and paper, mailing off the stories to publishers, paying the postage, and not incidentally collecting the fees, he gave his Brownies almost total credit for his productions.

Samuel Taylor Coleridge, a British poet, was accustomed to taking a sedative derived from opium (legal in those days). One afternoon after taking a dose he was reading and fell asleep over his book. The last words he read had been, "Here the Khan Kubla commanded a palace to be built." When Coleridge awoke some three hours later he had dreamed hundreds of lines of poetry, which he immediately set to writing down. The opening lines of this poem—one of the most famous of all time—are:

> In Xanadu did Kubla Khan
> A stately pleasure-dome decree:
> Where Alph, the sacred river, ran
> Through caverns measureless to man
> Down to a sunless sea.

Unfortunately for posterity, after writing only fifty-four lines of the two to three hundred he had dreamed, Coleridge was interrupted by a caller, whom he entertained for an hour. When he returned to complete the poem, he had lost all the rest of what he had dreamed! In his diary he noted that it had disappeared "like images on the surface of a stream." Even so, he had written a masterpiece. This true story, however, emphasizes the need to record dreams upon awakening, a subject we will take up in chapters 5 and 6.

Not only artists and writers give their dreams credit for their ideas and inspirations, but many scientists as well (as we saw in the examples of Bohr and Einstein). Psychologist Eliot D. Hutchinson reports numerous cases of scientists receiving information through dreams and says of dreams that "by them we can see more clearly the specific mechanism of intuitive thought," and that "a large number of thinkers with whom I have had direct contact admit that they dream more or less constantly about their work, especially if it is exceptionally baffling . . . they often extract useful conceptions."

I personally can attest to this statement, as it mirrors my own experience writing books. For example, when I began work on this book about dreams, I noticed that my dream production immediately *doubled;* and I have had Stevenson's experience of "little people," whom I call my "elves," and whom I write about extensively in my book for teens called *Teen Astrology,* telling about how they came to my rescue when I was quite stuck (see chapter 9, pages 249–252 in that book).

One of the most astonishing as well as fascinating stories is that of Hermann V. Hilprecht, a professor of Assyrian at the University of Pennsylvania in the late 1800s. It seems to be a characteristic of those who receive dream help that they have recently been working long and hard and are frustrated. In Hilprecht's case, he was working late one evening in 1893, attempting to decipher the cuneiform characters on drawings of two small fragments of agate. He thought they belonged to Babylonian finger rings, and he had tentatively assigned one fragment to the so-called Cassite period of 1700 B.C.E. However, he couldn't classify the second fragment. And he wasn't at all sure about the first either. He finally gave up his efforts at about midnight and went straight to bed—and had the following dream, which was his "astounding discovery."

Hilprecht dreamed of a priest of pre-Christian Nippur, several thousand years ago, who led the professor into the treasure chamber of the temple and showed him the originals, telling him just how the fragments fitted in, all in great detail. Although the dream was long and involved, Hilprecht remembered it all and in the morning told it to his wife. In his words: "Next morning . . . I examined the fragments once more in the light of these disclosures, and to my astonishment found all the details of the dream precisely verified in so far as the means of verification were in my hands."

Up until then, Hilprecht had been working only with drawings. Now he traveled to the museum in Constantinople where the actual agate fragments were kept and discovered that they fitted together perfectly, unlocking the secret of a three-thousand-year-old mystery by means of a dream!

How did this happen? Clairvoyance? Magic? Who was the priest?

How was it that Hilprecht seemed to make contact in a dream with someone who had lived so long before him? We will never know the answers to these questions; but we do know from the professor's own words that this is exactly what happened to him. (It makes you wonder whether Professor Hilprecht was in the habit of paying attention to his dreams!)

No doubt one of the most famous dream sources of scientific discovery was experienced by the German chemist Friedrich August Kekulé, when he was attempting to understand and model the molecular structure of benzene. Like Professor Hilprecht, Kekulé had been searching for the answer for many years and was totally immersed in the problem. He told of a dream he had while he napped in front of his fireplace one frigid night in 1865:

> Again the atoms were juggling before my eyes. . . . My mind's eye, sharpened by repeated sights of a similar kind, could not distinguish larger structures of different forms and in long chains, many of them close together; everything was moving in a snake-like and twisting manner. Suddenly, what was this? One of the snakes got hold of its own tail and the whole structure was mockingly twisting in front of my eyes. As if struck by lightning, I awoke.

This dream led Kekulé directly to the discovery of the structure of benzene, which is a closed carbon ring. A dream had presented a realization that served to revolutionize modern chemistry. Later, reporting his discovery to his colleagues at a scientific convention in 1890, he remarked, "Let us learn to dream, gentlemen, and then we may perhaps find the truth." Not the sort of comment one generally expects from a scientist!

Here is the story of another scientist. Otto Loewi, who won the 1936 Nobel Prize in Psychology and Medicine for his discovery of how the human nervous system works, credited this discovery to a dream. Prior to Loewi, scientists had assumed that the body's nervous impulses were the result of electrical waves. However, in 1903 Loewi had the intuition that a *chemical* transmission was actually responsible. But he had no way to prove his theory, so he set the idea aside for many years. Then, in 1920, he had the following dream:

> The night before Easter Sunday of that year I awoke, turned on the light, and jotted down a few notes on a tiny slip of thin paper. Then I fell asleep again. It occurred to me at six o'clock in the morning that during the night I had written down something most important, but I was unable to decipher the scrawl. The next night, at three o'clock, the idea returned. It was the design of an experiment to determine whether or not the hypothesis of chemical transmission that I had uttered seventeen years ago was correct. I got up immediately, went to the laboratory and performed a simple experiment on a frog's heart according to the nocturnal design. . . . Its results became the foundation of the theory of chemical transmission of the nervous impulse.

Interestingly, Loewi had previously performed a similar experiment, which combined in his dreaming mind with the new idea, creating the successful result. This is an excellent example of the ability of dreams to combine with previous dreams, or with actual events, to produce fertile new ground.

Be a Dream Explorer

"From time immemorial, people have used dreams in ways that benefited their waking lives. The more you learn to interact with your dream world, the more you integrate your total personality. Truly, this is a realm of magic and mystery, but one well worth exploring. Those who go fearlessly into the caverns of the night can return with untold treasure—and, intrepid explorers all, discover new territory in the vast, as-yet-unexplored continent of the human mind."

M. J. Abadie, *Your Psychic Potential*

These are some of the stories of famous people who have used dreams to solve problems, enhance creativity, and even make money and win important prizes. They are all evidence of the vast human ability to make use of dreams. As you draw upon your own dream life and develop skills in both dreaming and interpreting your dreams, you will become an advanced teen dreamer. Think of your dreams as a school where you are continually learning new skills and developing new aptitudes, reaching ever higher levels of achievement.

As you pay conscious attention to your dreams, and then use your dream symbols in your waking life, you will be integrating yourself, creating the greatest artwork of your life: your whole and unique Self.

A Short History of Dreaming

Dreams, it seems, have fascinated the entire human race from earliest times. And until quite recently, most cultures have set great store by dreams. For example, in ancient Egypt the high priests used dreams for prophecies. There still exists a papyrus book of dreams dating back approximately 3,500 years in which dream symbols are interpreted, proving that the Egyptians took their dreams seriously.

In ancient Greece, people believed that dreams were a direct contact with the gods. One of the principal uses of dreams was for healing. Sick people went to special temples that were dedicated to dreaming as a curative method. There, a physician would help to induce a dream, which the physician would then interpret as a guide to the treatment of the ailment, and its cause as well. In modern times, the father of psychoanalysis, Sigmund Freud, drew upon the writings of Artemidorus, a Greek who lived in the second century B.C.E. whom Freud much admired. Artemidorus's books have been preserved for over two thousand years and were in constant use as references before the scientific revolution put dreams into the category of "unimportant nonsense."

At the time of the Italian Renaissance, when rational thinking was beginning to come to the fore, dreams began to be dismissed as triv-

ial by-products of sleep. William Shakespeare denounced dreams as "the children of an idle brain." (On the other hand, he wrote eloquently on the nature of dreams in his play *Hamlet!*) John Dryden, an English philosopher, dismissed dreams as the result of indigestion or infection. The bias against dreams continued through the nineteenth century, when most people thought that dreams were caused by some external stimulus—such as a knock on the door making a person dream the house was being burglarized. Aside from such shallow interpretation, most ordinary people, doctors and philosophers, church fathers and professors, believed that dreams had no meaning and saw no need to heed them.

It took the work of Sigmund Freud to open people's eyes once more to the possibility of dreams being important and useful. Though Freud was obsessed with sexual meanings in dreams to the exclusion of all else, he performed a useful service with the publication of his book on dream interpretation. However, his narrow view held that dreams were mere "wish fulfillment" and a substitute for sexual satisfaction. Fortunately, one of his student colleagues, Carl Gustav Jung of Switzerland, disagreed with Freud and formulated a more comprehensive theory of dream analysis.

Jung researched the previously unstudied territory of the unconscious and came up with the idea of a *collective unconscious,* through which all people were connected by a common store of knowledge and experience that often revealed itself in dreams.

In his autobiography, *Memories, Dreams, Reflections,* Dr. Jung tells of a dream in which he was a guest at a garden party. Another guest was a woman from the town of Basel, a good friend of both Jung and his sister. In the dream, Jung says, he instinctively knew the woman from Basel would die. However, when he woke up he had no idea who the woman was in real life, though the dream was exceptionally vivid. He writes, "A few weeks later, I received news that a friend of mine had a fatal accident. I knew at once that she was the person I had seen in the dream but had been unable to identify."

CAN DREAMS COME TRUE?

In 1953, in order to test the possibility of ESP through dreaming—that is, dreams that predict the future or contact others telepathically—a New York psychiatrist named Montague Ulman designed an experiment that involved using a "sender" and a "receiver."

In this experiment, Ulman attached electrodes of an electroencephalograph (a machine that records brain waves) to the person acting as the receiver. This person would then go to sleep in one room.

The "sender" was placed in a different room. When the machine indicated the brain wave pattern that showed the receiver had fallen asleep, the sender opened a sealed envelope that contained a "target" image and concentrated fully on the picture in an attempt to influence the receiver's dream.

Once, when Ulman himself was acting as the sender, his thoughts strayed from the target image and he began to think about the book *Spartacus*, which had been made into a movie. The person acting as the receiver dreamed about the movie! Although his results were not all this successful, experiences such as this convinced Ulman that dream ESP was deserving of more research. So in 1962, with Stanley Krippner, he opened a dream laboratory in Brooklyn at Maimonides Medical Center. Although the two men's experiments continued to produce mixed results, Ulman felt the experiments proved at least the existence of dream telepathy, though not its reliability.

Having experienced instances of ESP in my own dreams, I must concur with the doctors about its reality. Here is an example of a precognitive dream from my own files:

The Dream: I am taken to a place where seminars are being held. Someone tells me that this is the same place that B. (a psychic healer friend of mine) studied. I peek around the corner and hear a man say, "Abadie is doing rocks."

I woke up feeling there was significance for me in "rocks," but at the time I couldn't figure out what it might be. Still, the word hung in my mind. A year later, I began working with crystals both for healing and telepathy.

The Nature of Sleep

What is sleep exactly? Although we know that all creatures that live sleep, and although science has diligently studied sleep in many sleep laboratories around the world, sleep itself—and its by-product, dreams—remains something of a mystery.

As I mentioned, you spend about a third of your life sleeping. If you have a life span of seventy-five years, you'll be asleep for twenty-five of those years. Imagine! Yet, despite the prevalence and common experience of sleep, only recently did science begin to understand what it is all about.

Although *dreaming* and its causes are still a matter for speculation, brain wave studies provide important information about sleep itself. In a normal night, a person passes through four different stages of sleep, identifiable by brain wave patterns, eye movements, and muscle tension.

In the first stage, the pattern of the brain waves goes from what is known as *beta*, or normal waking consciousness, to *alpha*, the first step into sleep. The beta phase is 13 to 26 cps (cycles per second, the speed of the oscillations in the brain wave cycle), during which you are awake and fully functioning, studying, working, socializing. The alpha phase is 8 to 13 cps, a state of deep relaxation during which you are still aware of your surroundings, whether with eyes open or closed. It is the precursor to sleep and the stage reached during light meditation. Alpha is the sort of somnolent state we might go into on a long train ride when we have been staring out the window at a monotonous landscape for hours and are lulled by boredom and inactivity.

During the alpha stage, heart and pulse rates slow down, blood pressure drops slightly, and so does temperature. Your muscles are in a relaxed condition and you experience mental "drifting." Images described as *hypnogogic* may float through your mind, seemingly unrelated to anything or else variations of what you were thinking or doing just before going to bed. These hypnogogic images can be vivid, as if drug-induced. Sometimes these images are quite meaningful and may startle you back to the beta state. When this happens, you may experience your muscles jumping back to the ready-to-go stage, a common happening that is called the *myoclonic jerk*.

"Dreaming liberates perception, enlarging the scope of what can be perceived."

Carlos Castaneda,
The Art of Dreaming

Stage three is called *theta* and is represented by 4 to 8 cps, the same rate you display during periods of intense daydreaming (when you can actually forget where you are) or deep meditation. This stage of abstractedness is sometimes called a *brown study*. In the theta state, you are neither fully awake nor fully asleep. Yet you are in a light slumber, and, if not disturbed, you will fall asleep. The brain wave pattern of theta is characterized by rapid bursts of brain activity. Sleep researchers believe that theta is truly a sleep state, but when disrupted out of this state many subjects report that they were not asleep but merely "thinking."

Researchers believe that it is during the theta stage that most dreams occur. Dreams are recognizable to an observer by what is called rapid eye movement, or REM. The eyeballs move back and forth like someone watching a tennis match under their closed lids. Researchers originally discovered REM by watching cats sleep, and if you observe either a cat or a person sleeping, you will notice their eyes moving back and forth. A cat or dog may twitch as if running, but during REM a human's muscles are virtually paralyzed. The period of REM ordinarily lasts for several minutes at a time, switching on and off. If you awaken during a REM period, you will most likely remember your dreams easily and in great detail.

The last stage is *delta;* at 0 to 4 cps, it is the slowest and is evident during the deepest part of the sleep cycle. This is the state when you are totally out and even a ringing telephone or alarm clock may not wake you. Teens often experience this deepest level of sleep in the early morning hours, which is why they are often hard to wake up for school. Teens actually do better when allowed to sleep late: you function better, learn better, and generally feel better when you are able to "sleep yourself out." It's unfortunate that teens are often mandated an early rising time for school or even before-school activities, such as sports practice. It's not only *how much* you sleep, apparently, but also *when* you get your sleep that counts.

People awakened from the delta stage of sleep will feel disoriented and only half awake, and they will want nothing more than to go back to sleep. If, for example, a need to visit the bathroom wakes you from a delta sleep, you may bump into the furniture or the walls, even though you know your way around. During delta, there are no eye movements. It is also the time that sleepwalking occurs. As most everyone knows, a sleepwalker can move around unerringly, as if awake, and should be left alone unless he or she is in danger. If not awakened, sleepwalkers almost always make their way back to bed without a problem, and when they do wake up they have no memory of their nighttime excursions.

An average complete sleep cycle lasts about three hours. For the first hour and a half of the cycle the sleeper moves from a waking state to light sleep to REM sleep to deep dreamless sleep. The cycle reverses itself in the second half, returning upward (so to speak) from the deep sleep of delta to the lighter theta-alpha stages. As brain activity rises, so do blood pressure, pulse, and temperature. In warm weather, you may be awakened by feeling hot as your body temperature returns to normal. This is always a clue that you are in the process of waking up, and it's a good sign to be aware of so that you will focus on your dreams and be ready to take notes on them.

Every night you go through three or four complete sleep cycles of ninety minutes each. The first REM period of the night lasts five to ten minutes. During each cycle, the REM is repeated, lasting longer as the night progresses, while the time between the cycles gets shorter. Your last REM can be as long as an hour, and this is prime dreamtime with excellent chances for good recall of your dreams. What this means in practical terms is that, if you sleep for seven hours straight, half of your dreamtime will occur during the two hours before you wake up in the morning. *An additional hour of sleep will give you an additional hour of dreaming!* This is a powerful argument for getting to bed early enough to get eight hours of continuous sleep. Of course, these figures are based on laboratory averages and may not hold true for every person—you are an individual and will sleep and dream in

your own way. I have found that I dream twice as much as the average reported by sleep studies, sometimes with less sleep than the average, sometimes with more.

None of these states of consciousness—beta, alpha, theta, delta—are foreign to us. We cycle through all four of them during the course of twenty-four hours, slipping in and out of them, mostly without noticing. For example, during normal beta wakefulness, you may drift off into a daydream or reverie, thinking about tonight's date or tomorrow's picnic, and enter the alpha phase for a while. The phone rings, or a friend speaks to you, and you snap back into the beta state.

Or you could be driving your car along a monotonous route with little to pay attention to and slip for a few moments into the theta phase (lots of people fall asleep at the wheel for a few seconds and then quickly recover) only to flip back into beta as you see a sharp curve up ahead or hear another car honking. Everyone has had the experience of "dropping off" for a couple of seconds during ordinary everyday activities (or, perhaps, lack of activity).

For those who want to pursue dream studies, it's important to pay attention to these alpha-theta states. There is a twilight zone where you are neither asleep nor awake but are alert to slight disturbances. It's here you may catch a dream as it is forming, and it is in this state that you are best able to give yourself instructions for remembering your dreams-to-come and for "programming" dreams to fulfill specific purposes.

Use the following exercise to track your own personal sleep patterns. Following the format given here, keep a record of your sleep habits for two weeks in order to prepare for the exercises throughout this book. You'll find out a lot about your sleep needs, when you dream, and your level of recall. Over time, even from day to day, you may find differences that are worth noting. Then, if you want to continue the process, record your sleep habits in a separate notebook.

Teen Dream Exercise

Sleep Habits

Fill in the accompanying chart for two weeks, noting when you went to bed, whether you fell asleep at once or tossed and turned, what time you woke up in the morning, if you woke during the night, what was on your mind before sleeping, what and when you ate, any TV or other presleep activity, and anything else you think would relate to your personal sleep patterns.

WEEK ONE

Sunday: Date_____

Bedtime:_____ Waking time:_____

Presleep Notes:_____

_____

Postsleep Notes:_____

_____

Monday: Date_____

Bedtime:_____ Waking time:_____

Presleep Notes:_____

_____

Postsleep Notes:_____

_____

Tuesday: Date_____

Bedtime:_____ Waking time:_____

Presleep Notes:_____

_____

Postsleep Notes:_____

_____

Wednesday: Date_____

Bedtime:_____ Waking time:_____

Presleep Notes: _____

_____

Postsleep Notes: _____

_____

Thursday: Date_____

Bedtime:_____ Waking time:_____

Presleep Notes: _____

_____

Postsleep Notes: _____

_____

Friday: Date_____

Bedtime:_____ Waking time:_____

Presleep Notes: _____

_____

Postsleep Notes: _____

_____

Saturday: Date_____

Bedtime:_____ Waking time:_____

Presleep Notes: _____

_____

Postsleep Notes: _____

_____

Week Two

Sunday: Date_____

Bedtime:_____ Waking time:_____

Presleep Notes:_____

_____

Postsleep Notes:_____

_____

Monday: Date_____

Bedtime:_____ Waking time:_____

Presleep Notes:_____

_____

Postsleep Notes:_____

_____

Tuesday: Date_____

Bedtime:_____ Waking time:_____

Presleep Notes:_____

_____

Postsleep Notes:_____

_____

Wednesday: Date_____

Bedtime:_____ Waking time:_____

Presleep Notes: _____

_____

Postsleep Notes:_____

_____

Thursday: Date_____

Bedtime:_____ Waking time:_____

Presleep Notes: _____

_____

Postsleep Notes:_____

_____

Friday: Date_____

Bedtime:_____ Waking time:_____

Presleep Notes: _____

_____

Postsleep Notes:_____

_____

Saturday: Date_____

Bedtime:_____ Waking time:_____

Presleep Notes: _____

_____

Postsleep Notes:_____

_____

The richness of the hidden vale of dreams is exemplified in the following fairy tale about twelve princesses whose slippers were discovered to be in shreds each morning.

The Dream Weaver

Once upon a time a king had twelve beautiful daughters, each of whom managed to ruin a perfectly good pair of satin slippers every single night. With so many daughters to feed, clothe, and provide for (each one had to have a dowry, or treasure to give to her future husband), the king of this otherwise happy land was in despair. He was a good king and loved his beautiful daughters, but he was not a rich man. The expense of having to pay the shoemaker every day to make each princess a new pair of shoes was quite bothersome to him.

Not only that, but he was vexed at the mystery of the worn-out shoes, which had been brand new only the morning before. Questioning his teenage daughters had proved fruitless. (We all know that teen girls like to keep secrets from their fathers.) None would tell him what they did every night to ruin their shoes. And since they were always locked into their night chambers behind guarded doors, he was baffled. In fact, he became so upset that he neglected the business of his kingdom, which brought in complaints. Finally, his wife suggested that he send out a proclamation offering to give half his kingdom and the choice of his daughters as a bride to any knight who could discover the princesses' secret.

Many knights applied for the job, showing up proudly at the castle on their fine horses, ready to do battle with the unknown and earn themselves half a kingdom and a princess for a wife. But they all failed and went away poorer than when they had arrived. Although each knight was locked inside the princesses' rooms at night with the girls, each morning the knight was found sound asleep and—once again—all the princesses' slippers were in tatters.

Finally, one fine day when the king was on the verge of a nervous breakdown, a new knight, in shining white armor, rode up to the castle on a magnificent snorting white charger and threw down his gauntlet to the challenge.

Immensely relieved to have a new ally, the king ordered his cooks to feed him an excellent dinner. Then he locked him in with the princesses, who seemed glad to have a male visitor and generously offered him a glass of wine—which was, of course, drugged. This was how they had disposed of all of the previous knights and kept their secret.

The knight accepted the wine but only pretended to drink it, and then he pretended to fall into a deep sleep. When the entire castle was fast asleep, the twelve princesses arose from their couches and dressed themselves in beautiful ball gowns made of silk and ribbons. The knight watched all of this with great interest from slitted eyes; but the princesses did not notice at all as they giggled and talked about their coming adventure. Each put on her pair of new shoes. Then they entered a secret passageway that led underground from behind their closet.

Now the knight wrapped himself in a magic cloak that made him invisible, which his mother had woven of her dreams. He followed the princesses down, down, down, into a fabulous underground world, filled with jewels and treasures of every description. At the bottom of the long winding staircase was a lake, with twelve little boats waiting at the shore. Each princess stepped into a boat, and each boat sailed by itself across the mirrorlike surface of the underground lake. Just as the last princess, the youngest, was about to embark in her boat, the knight stepped into the boat behind her. Feeling his weight, she called out to her sisters, already sailing across the crystal water, but as they could not see anything unusual, they told her to come along and stop being a silly goose.

On the opposite shore, the princesses disembarked into the waiting arms of twelve handsome troubadours. The princesses and their escorts danced their way through a series of bejeweled gardens: the first was paved with pink marble and the trees and bushes grew rubies; the second, floored with amber, was filled with flowers made of emeralds; in the third they danced on shining silver tiles and every tree held blossoms of sapphire; the fourth and last garden glittered underfoot with solid gold and the couples danced with the light from thousands of blossoms of twinkling diamonds. The knight could hardly believe his eyes as he followed the troupe of dancers from garden to splendid garden.

All night the princesses and their troubadours whirled and spun in the

jewel-encrusted underground gardens to the strains of celestial music which seemed to come from everywhere and nowhere at the same time. Just before dawn, the eldest princess called the sisters together and warned, "Hurry, it is almost light and we must be in our beds before the knight awakens and the guard unlocks the door."

Knowing the marvels he experienced would never be believed without evidence, the knight plucked a flowering twig from each of the four gardens and hid them in his magic cloak as he passed through, following the princesses. The youngest heard the snap of a bough breaking, but looking around she again saw nothing out of the ordinary, so she hurried to catch up with her sisters. As the princesses stepped into the little boats the knight noticed that the graceful slippers on their feet had been danced to satin shreds.

When the boats reached the other shore, the knight—still concealed in his cloak of woven dreams—raced up the long stairway ahead of the princesses to the sleeping chambers, took off his cloak, lay down, and pretended to be fast asleep. When the princesses returned, they tossed their ruined shoes into a heap and climbed into their beds.

Later that morning, the king summoned the knight to the throne room and demanded to know if he had discovered the princesses' secret. The knight told all he had seen, to the amazement of his host and the astonishment of the princesses, who insisted he was lying. But when he unwrapped his cloak and presented the king with the jeweled twigs of ruby, emerald, sapphire, and diamonds, the eldest princess confessed all to her father, who was so pleased to learn the answer to the mystery that he decreed that the princesses could have all the new slippers they desired, if only they would share with him the marvels of their wondrous nocturnal world.

And the knight—whom did he choose to be his bride? The eldest sister.

In this little tale we find a perfect metaphor for the dream experience. The princesses are our nonlinear, nonrational faculties that, at the onset of night, slip away to a private realm of inexhaustible treasures and fantastic adventures. That there are twelve princesses suggests the twelve hours of the night. The knights who failed are all those

who don't remember their dreams—the rational-minded who think there is nothing else in the world except what one can measure with the five gross senses. The knight who succeeds is the one whose mother wove him a cloak of her dreams, enabling him to enter the magical realm of the princesses and return with proof of having been there. In other words, he is not afraid of the feminine, nonrational side of life and can walk its ways in safety.

My take on his choice of the eldest princess as his bride (it's usually the youngest daughter who gets the prince) is that she represents the wisdom of the feminine realm. The king is the masculine counterpart, the waking consciousness, which is incomplete without knowledge of our nocturnal dream wanderings in the jeweled lands hidden beneath the castle of ordinary everyday reality. This waking consciousness longs to connect with its other half in order to feel whole and complete.

2

Dream Explorers around the World

"Dreams count. The Spirits have compassion for us and have guided us."

PROVERB OF THE NATIVE AMERICAN CREE

In chapter 1, we considered the stories of famous individuals who received surprising help from their dreams. In this chapter, we are going to discuss those peoples throughout the world who have been accomplished Dream Explorers.

DREAMERS OF THE FORESTS AND THE PLAINS

Among the world's fine Dream Explorers were the Native American peoples who populated the American continent before the arrival of the Europeans. Fortunately, unlike some ancient dreamers whose ways have been largely lost or are only available from myth and story, many Native Americans are alive today, direct descendants of their ancient ancestors. While some of their traditions have been lost or altered, many have been carefully preserved—often in secret—and handed down to those who followed the keepers of the traditions.

It is estimated that around one million Native Americans were spread out over the vast territory of what is now the United States when the first European settlers arrived. These native peoples lived in all parts of the territory, with its differing climate zones and geographies, and followed all different ways of life. For example, the

Iroquois of the Northeast lived by hunting deer and growing corn. In the far northern regions, the Ojibwa hunted caribou and elk, while farther south tribes such as the Cherokee cultivated tobacco and were known as Mound Builders.

On the wet and mild Northwest coast, the site of present-day Oregon and Washington State, the Kwakutl lived plentiful lives, feeding themselves on the salmon that were abundant in the cold streams of the region. They were skilled fishermen, and the men even hunted whales in the open ocean while the women of the tribes gathered the plentiful berries and other plant foodstuffs. Known for their intricate woodcarvings made from the wood of the cedar tree, these people had a fine way of life.

Meanwhile, in the hot, dry desert of the Southwest, the Pueblo lived settled lives in huge terraced villages of adobe. They farmed various crops and raised sheep for meat. Some tribes continued to practice simple gathering techniques, picking edible wild plants wherever they grew and hunting wild game for meat. Some, like the Navajo, wove beautiful blankets and created stunning jewelry from silver and turquoise.

As white settlers came across the continent, they changed some of the ways of the native population. The Spanish expedition in the 1600s introduced horses, which had previously been unknown here, and soon some tribes, like the Cheyenne, had acquired horses and were breeding them, eventually migrating to the great plains with their animals to hunt the buffalo that roamed there in great herds.

As the new settlers continued to move westward, they encountered even more varied ways of native life. The Shoshone, a nomadic tribe of what is now the northwestern United States, lived mainly on a diet of acorns and seeds, which they gathered in season and stored for winter use.

In the midst of all these differences in ways of life and widely varying customs and culture, language and beliefs, there were some things shared by all the Native Americans, and among them was this: a reverence for dreams and knowledge of the importance of dream life.

In many earlier cultures, the distinction between dreams and waking life was not as distinct as it is now. Dreaming and waking life were closely connected, each one flowing into the other in a natural manner. We find an example of this in a native culture that is still following its traditional ways: the Naskapi, who inhabit a frozen territory in northeastern Canada. Today, there are only about three hundred Naskapi tribal members left, but they carry on as their ancestors before them did. They have no organized government or institutional structure, and they follow no prescribed religion. They live by hunting caribou and bear. The tribe maintains its rich spiritual tradition, which is heavily influenced by dreaming.

In his book *Synchronicity*, David Peat comments, "Central to the life of the Naskapi is the Big Dream, in which the hunter goes on the trail, meets friends, and locates herds of caribou." The Swiss psychologist Carl Jung, whom we learned of in chapter 1, identified *big dreams* and *little dreams*. A big dream is an important guide and usually easily recognizable both by its vividness and by being almost totally recalled.

When the Naskapi hunter-dreamer wakes from his Big Dream, which he has deliberately sought, he immediately begins to drum and chant to alert others of the tribe that he has had a Big Dream and now knows where the best hunting grounds are. His music-making is also intended to communicate to the spirits of the forest animals, who are expected to help the hunters find and kill the caribou. It is important to note that native tribes *never* kill for "sport," but only for food, and they always eat what they kill. The idea of killing a valuable food animal just for the "fun of it" horrifies them, as well it should horrify us. All tribal peoples have some ceremony to ask the animal to sacrifice itself for their lives and to honor its death in the cycle of life. They approach the hunt with reverence for all life on the earth and ask the spirits to forgive them for the kill.

According to Naskapi belief, a hunter will become a Great Hunter, able to have clear and powerful dreams, only if he respects the

"What we find as soon as we place ourselves in the perspective of the religious man of the archaic societies is that . . . the existence of the world 'means' something, 'wants to say' something, that the world is neither mute nor opaque, that it is not an inert thing without purpose or significance. For religious man, the cosmos lives and speaks."

Mircea Eliade,
The Sacred and the Profane

animals he hunts and shares his kill with the members of his tribe. If he neglects or violates this covenant with Life, his dreams will desert him and he will no longer be a successful dreamer-hunter.

The key to this way of life in which dream, dreamer, and waking activity are all intimately connected is the recognition that there are *patterns* in nature. It is the hunter-dreamer's job to put himself in harmony with these patterns. Peat notes, "The Naskapi live in a world of meaningful pattern in which no distinction exists between what we have come to call mind and matter."

In native cultures, dreams were often part of the religious system, providing a method for the dreamer to contact the Great Spirit, or the spirits of animals and plants, in order to gain power over them or to seek their permission to find and use them. Dreams were also an important part of the social system. Interpreters of dreams were the psychologists of the culture, using dreams to solve mental and emotional problems. Also, dreams were used to predict the future and to guide the tribe's social life. If, for example, a tribe was nomadic, a master dreamer (called a *shaman* or *medicine man*) would be called upon to dream the best new location.

Native Americans had specific rituals to get rid of nightmares and to promote dreams that were useful both to the individual and to the tribe. Healing was another function of dreaming, as it was in ancient Greece. A dream could indicate the nature of the illness and suggest its cure.

These are only a few examples out of the intricate, complex system of dreaming that the tribes used. Although many of their practices are not applicable to our lives today, we can still learn much from these dreamers. The primary point is this:

Those who believe their dreams are important to their waking lives will have dreams that are useful and will remember them.

According to Patricia Garfield in *Creative Dreaming,* an unusual characteristic of the Native American dreamer-hunter, shaman, or medicine man was that he or she was required to dream each step of an activity to be undertaken, with specific characters (dream friends), a specific location, and a specific timeline of operation. This means that four dreams were necessary to fulfill the function. For example, if a tribe was going to war, the head warrior had to dream all of the steps before he could be appointed as the leader of the war party. He had to know exactly where to go, how to get there, how many opposing enemies he would meet, and how many would be killed or injured on each side.

Failing this, he could not be a leader. Anthropologists who have studied the dream habits of Native Americans believe that this kind of dream could not be faked. To be exposed as a faker was a fate worse than death!

DREAMERS OF THE JUNGLE

Now let us cross the world to a vastly different place and investigate the dreams of a people known as the Senoi, for whom dreams are perhaps the most important part of their lives. Imagine this scene:

The sun is peeking over the horizon, spreading its beams to wake all sleepers to a new day. In every household of the Senoi people of Malaysia, the women are preparing food, usually tropical fruits, as the first meal of the day. Outside in the jungle the animals are already up and about, making various noises—an elephant trumpets to his mate, monkeys chatter and leap about the rain forest trees, birds call in different tones—high, low, shrill, melodious. The forest is alive with movement and sound.

Inside the dwelling, the group contains quite a few relatives other than the main family—uncles, aunts, cousins, and visitors—and each person has an assigned place at the long table. The leaf platters of fruit and other food are passed along for all to help themselves. Then comes the moment all have been awaiting. The father speaks softly, asking the question that is the beginning of each day, "What did you dream last night?"

Thus begins another day for the Senoi family that is repeated in every

"Hunting is a great teacher of life. It is a way of harnessing natural passions, that intensity of experiences [we have in the teen years]. Learning to guide our passions with ethics and values moves us into adulthood. When you learn to hunt in an ethical manner, showing respect to animals, eating what you kill, taking only what you need, and giving to nature by helping preserve wildlife habitat, preventing pollution, and reporting poachers, you will not only be a good hunter, you will be a good citizen, whose values will inspire other people to care about nature. Mastering a lethal weapon . . . is a sign that you are a responsible person."

James A. Swan, Ph. D.,
The Power of Place: Sacred Ground in Natural and Human Environments

Hold fast to dreams
For if dreams die
Life is a broken-winged bird
That cannot fly.
Hold fast to dreams
For when dreams go
Life is a barren field
Frozen with snow.

Langston Hughes,
The Dream Keeper

household. And, in turn, each tells his or her dreams. No one, not even the youngest child, will reply, "I didn't dream anything," or "I don't remember," for dreaming is too important to be ignored or forgotten. It is the cornerstone of Senoi life.

The Senoi are a large and primitive tribe (by modern standards) who live in the mountainous jungles of Malaysia. They have become quite well known as anthropologists have studied their ways and their unique use of dreams, and have published their findings. Anyone studying dreams knows about the Senoi. They are estimated to consist of approximately twelve hundred people who live in three groupings on the Malay Peninsula, some more primitive than others due to their isolation from modern Malaysia with its more sophisticated populations.

Living in communal units of extended families, they occupy what are known as *longhouses*, aptly described by the name, that they build to last a few years. Physically, they are attractive—tall, slim, with light brown skin and fine, wavy hair. Inside the longhouse, each family has its own space for living and cooking, but the entire group living in the longhouse acts like a small village, using the central aisle as Main Street. As a group, they work to farm a cleared area of the jungle with a small variety of edible crops—pumpkins, bananas, yams, rice, and tapioca. When the soil has exhausted its fertility, after four or five years of farming, they move on to another location and build a new longhouse.

Other than planting and harvesting their crops, the mostly vegetarian Senoi also hunt small animals and fish by a unique method, which involves crushing a fruit containing a juice that acts like a sedative on fish. They squeeze this into the stream and then just wait for the stunned fish to float to the top where they can be netted or just lifted out by hand. These few activities leave them with lots of spare time, which they use mainly in reporting, interpreting, discussing, and preparing for the next night's dreaming.

Children begin to report their dreams at an early age, around the meal table, as soon as they can talk. Each child is praised by the adults for reporting a dream and instructed—if necessary—about how to prepare for another dream. For example, if a child has a nightmare and dreams a wild beast is chasing her, she is instructed to confront the animal in the next dream and either drive it away or make friends with it. Nightmares soon cease as the child learns the technique.

After the morning meal, many of the tribe's members gather in the village's council place, where they continue discussing dreams. This is their "work." All activities from birth to death and everything in between—illness, food crops, needs, solutions to problems—are determined by the dreams of individual tribe members. Everyone tells his or her dream to the whole group, which then decides what to do with the dream's content. Each council member has the right to give his or her own interpretation of each dream, and general discussion follows as the significance of each dream symbol is decided upon. If several members agree on the meaning of a single dream, it becomes a group project.

The Senoi people live their entire lives by dream interpretation and dream activity. Most of the activities of their everyday lives are determined by these dream discussions. Decisions about the group are made based on their dreams. When and where to move to a different location is a result of dream interpretation and discussion among the group. Creative activity is high, and adults will help children to make objects they have seen in a dream. Many Senoi dream quite creatively—and then they design and make costumes, paintings, music, dance, and songs that they have dreamed up. Except for the few hours needed to gather and prepare food, they spend their time acting out their dream-inspirations of all sorts. A musical people, the Senoi enhance their dream life with the playing of handmade

The Senoi Rules of Dreaming

The author of *Creative Dreaming*, Patricia Garfield, studied the Senoi extensively, relying mainly on the written material of Kilton Stewart, an American anthropologist and psychoanalyst who lived with the Senoi for several years along with British anthropologist Herbert Noone. She found that there are some general rules, the first being "confront and conquer danger." The following imagined scene, which supposes that a child reports a dream of being chased by a tiger, is an adaptation from Garfield's book.

Child: I dreamed I was chased by a tiger last night.

Parent: What did you do?

Child: I ran as fast as I could. He kept getting closer and closer. I couldn't run any faster. I woke up very frightened.

Parent: It was good you had that dream, but you made a mistake. The tigers you see in the jungle in the daytime can hurt you, and you may need to run, but the tigers you see in your dreams can only hurt you if you run from them. They will continue to chase you only so long as you are afraid of them. The next time you are chased by a tiger in a dream you must turn around and face the tiger. If it attacks, you must fight back.

Child: But what if it is too big and strong for me?

Parent: Then call on your dream friends for help, but fight along until help arrives. Never run away from something that attacks or frightens you in a dream. Always confront the danger.

The second rule Garfield discovered is "Advance toward pleasure in a dream." She says the child is encouraged to seek pleasurable sensations, including sexual ones, in dreams. The third rule is "Achieve a positive outcome." For example, children are encouraged to do such things as turn a dream of falling off a cliff into a happy experience of flying. As Garfield comments, "This is surely a sophisticated 'power of positive thinking' approach from these 'primitive' people."

Lastly, the best possible outcome is to obtain a gift from one of the dream characters to bring back to share with his family and the tribe. We will discuss more about this extraordinary technique in chapter 4.

lutes, flutes, gongs, and drums, with which to accompany communal singing, a preparation for the night's dreaming. When the sun goes down, the jungle gets quieter (though it is always a bit noisy), and the families retire for another night of dreaming—to sleep, to dream, to wake, to tell their dreams, and to live another dream-directed day.

The Senoi people have been able to preserve their traditional ways because they live in a remote and all but inaccessible terrain. Researchers have to use helicopters or riverboats to reach them. In the dense jungle, thick with trees, climbing plants, underground trailing roots, and a variety of vines, ferns, mosses, and thick ropelike creepers, it's often necessary to use a machete or other type of blade to cut a path. Malaria is a constant threat to Western researchers, but the Senoi have a natural immunity to this disease.

Despite their sophisticated use of dreams and the ability to control the content of their dreams (we'll discuss dream control in chapter 4), the Senoi are considered primitive or uncivilized by the scientific standards of our time. Though they do live simply with few material goods, they are far advanced in the use of dreams to guide their lives. Living as they do far from "civilized" society (a relative term!), they are still closely connected to their unconscious processes and have no trouble integrating waking life with dream life. In fact, they don't even consider that there is a difference between the two. It is all one flow of life.

"The myth is the public dream and the dream is the private myth."
Joseph Campbell,
The Power of Myth

The Senoi are a peaceful people and extremely cooperative with their fellows. Responsibilities, food, land, dreams, work, play, music—all are shared within the group. At the same time, each child is encouraged to develop individually, to dream his or her own dreams, and to participate in the life of the community as a respected member. There is no division—except that of the level of maturity—between children and adults. Everyone is considered of equal importance and everyone's dreams are listened to respectfully.

Perhaps as a result of this seamless cooperation and the lack of

Teen Dream Tip

By not being critical of any dream experience and using productive ways of handling negative dream images, you can convert the negative into positive, turn fear to courage, avoid danger, seek pleasure, and have a happy outcome. These in turn will carry over into your waking life.

"They say we have been here for sixty thousand years, but it is much longer. We have been here since the time before time began. We have come directly out of the Dreamtime of the Creative Ancestors. We have lived and kept the earth as it was on the First Day."

Aborginal tribal elder in
Voices of the First Day
by Robert Lawlor

a gap between the generations, these extraordinary people are free of the neuroses and other psychological problems that plague other, more "advanced" societies. Since their desire for possessions does not rule their lives, they don't spend their time working to accumulate more and more "things," finding their happiness and satisfaction in their experience of and use of dreams. And they use their time efficiently, with a minimum of energy spent on the necessities of shelter and food production. That way, they have the majority of their time available for their dream projects, some of which are quite large and involve the whole community. Although it cannot be proved, researchers are of the opinion that their use of dreams is the mainspring of their characteristics of cooperation and peacefulness.

Senoi children are especially cherished and from their earliest days are taught the tribe's dream techniques. Like children everywhere, they suffer from nightmares, but they are instructed carefully by their elders on a daily basis and soon learn to turn away monsters or wild beasts who may frighten them while dreaming. By the time they reach their teen years, nightmares are a thing of the past and they are producing dreams useful to their community.

THE "DREAMTIME" OF AUSTRALIA'S ABORIGINES

So far as we know, the Aborigines of Australia are the only culture to credit dreams with creation. Even today, Aboriginal tribespeople live each day connected to "the Dreaming," and base their lives and everyday activities on what they believe happened long ago, when their ancestors dreamed the world into being. In his book *Voices of the First Day*, the Australian author and artist Robert Lawlor says:

> The Australian Aboriginal culture is founded entirely on the remembrance of the origin of life. According to some recent evidence, their story of creation, along with the worldview it fostered, has survived for perhaps 150,000 years. The Aborigines refer to the forces and powers that created the

world as their Creative Ancestors. For them, our beautiful world could have been created perfect only in accordance with the power, wisdom, and intentions of these original ancestral beings. During the world-creating epoch called the Dreaming, the Ancestors moved across a barren, undifferentiated field in a manner similar to that of the Aboriginal people wandering across their vast countryside. The Ancestors traveled, hunted, made camp, fought, and loved, and in so doing they shaped a featureless field into a topographical landscape. Before their travels, they would sleep and dream the adventures and episodes of the following day. In this manner, moving from dreams to actions, the Ancestors made the ants, the grasshoppers, the emus, the crows, the parrots, the wallabies, the kangaroos, the lizards, the snakes, and all the foods and plants. They made all the natural elements, the sun, the moon, and the stars. They made humans, tribes, and clans. All these things were created by the Ancestors simultaneously, and each could transform into any of the others. A plant could become an animal, an animal a landform, a landform a man or woman. An ancestor could be both human and animal. Back and forth the transformations occurred as the adventures of the Dreamtime stories required. Everything was created from the same source—the dreamings and doings of the great Ancestors. All stages, phases, and cycles were present at once in the Dreamtime. As the world took shape and was filled with the species and varieties of the ancestral transformations, the Ancestors wearied and retired into the earth, the sky, the clouds, and the creatures, to reverberate like a potency within all they had created.

Though the stories vary somewhat from clan to clan, the Dreaming stories are a basic part of Aboriginal life throughout Australia. During the Dreamtime, the Ancestors "took innovative

"As with the events of waking experience, the images of our dreams offer an important glimpse into the workings of the deep psyche written in the language of symbolism and analogy. [For example, the Senoi child's dream of being chased by a tiger might represent a fear of becoming adult or fear of the powers of adults.] According to some traditions, however, dreams issue from a subtler level of consciousness than the phenomena of everyday life, and for that reason offer a decidedly more fluid look into the changing psychological condition of the soul than do waking events. According to esoteric Hindu teachings, dream symbolism offers insight into the emotional dimensions of our being."

Ray Grasse,
The Waking Dream

Darwin's Creation Myth

According to Robert Lawlor, Darwin's theory of evolution—the basic creation myth of our Western civilization for the past 150 years—is also only a story that cannot be proved. Says Lawlor, "While Darwin and his proponents claimed to have 'proved' his theory, it cannot be scientifically tested." Despite this, what we call Darwinism has become the unquestioned orthodox belief of both science and academic institutions. It is now the "lens through which all thinking about human origins is assessed. The edifices of modern life sciences are built on a belief in this story." And a somewhat grim story it is, a story that develops from seeing all of Nature as a set of mechanical laws, and ends up giving human beings the right to exploit all of creation for their own desires.

"You can provide yourself with the rewards for dreaming that our society does not give. Regard your own dreams as important and they will aid you."

Patricia Garfield,
Creative Dreaming

action and unprecedented risks, discovering as they went along customs, techniques, and behaviors that either helped to bring joy and order or precipitated pain, destruction, and disease. The lessons of life implicit in the stories were distilled into what the Aborigines called the Dreamtime Law and were reflected in the utter simplicity of the Aboriginal way of life," says Lawlor.

In the Dreamtime stories, all of creation was produced through the original Dreaming, and every created thing acts out of dreams. Entry into the larger world—of space and time, of universal laws and energies—was a result of dreaming.

Of course, the Dreamtime stories cannot be proved. All cultures have creation myths, and these myths have far-reaching effects on the people who believe them. What is unusual about the Australian Aborigines is that they live their daily lives in strict accordance with the dreams of their Ancestors as these have been passed down for all these thousands of years. In other words, for something like 150,000 years, the Aborigines have sustained their culture, living in harmony with nature as their mythology requires.

There is much for us to learn from the Dreamtime of Australia's Aborigines and their resulting way of life. For them, all of earth is the visible intelligence of the original creation. It is symbolic of the universal Dreaming, which brought it into being. Through dreams, the Aborigines receive the teachings of their Ancestors and celebrate them in song, dance, and ritual. The Great Dream contains within it all human dreams, and guides them. This view is similar to Dr. Jung's concept of the collective unconscious. Like the Senoi people, Aborigines derive creative ideas from their dreams, which are automatically linked to the Dreamtime of their Ancestors. A dream is like a pregnancy: inside the dreamer, new life is growing and will become manifest in the world in time. And, like new life, the developing mind, body, and spirit of young people—teens like yourself—change in relation to what they dream, since dreams are reflections of the true Self.

Modern Physics?

It is extremely interesting to note that both present-day quantum physics and modern psychology accept that there is a single universal force beneath the visible, tangible world. This modern view is a mirror image of the Aboriginal awareness that there is a single continuum underlying the Dreaming and the visible forms it has produced and continues to produce. Quantum physics theorizes that there is a universal field as the basis of all levels of energy and that all particles and rhythmic energies arise from this field continuum. Although the "field" remains a mystery (as does, for example, gravity), its effects are evident. Anyone can prove the existence of the magnetic field with a magnet and some iron filings, or the refrigerator door!

DREAM INCUBATION

As we learned earlier, the ancient Greeks induced dreams for healing. But they were not the only culture to use dreams to produce astonishing cures, or to use them for other purposes. The ancient Egyptians, Chinese, Japanese, Hebrews, and Indians all practiced the art of dream incubation. These ancient Dream Explorers did this by *expecting* to make contact with a god in their dream who would prescribe a cure, answer a question, or solve a problem. Naturally, it would be a god with whom the dreamer was already familiar. The gods are representative of what Dr. Jung calls *archetypes,* or basic patterns that already exist. It is Jung's theory that one of the deepest of human needs is to contact the archetypal level and interact with the figures that represent different energies.

For example, in addition to a healing god, there are other archetypal figures that appear all over the world, in dreams and through guided meditations or in the process of psychotherapy. There are mother and father archetypes, wise man and wise woman archetypes,

The Earth's Soul

William Gilbert, the founder of the modern science of magnetism, called the earth's magnetic field its soul. Today's earth scientists consider that the earth's magnetic field is an energy that is produced by the movements of the molten rock at the core of the earth's interior. Aborigines might say that magnetism is the voice of the earth's Dreaming.

"The dream itself is a rebellion against language—and against, ultimately, the restriction that any kind of expression seems to impose on truth."

Brenda Murphee,
Dreams Are Wiser than Men

and so on. The dream god, or a holy figure such as a Christian saint, is an archetypal energy wearing the mask of a particular culture.

With few exceptions, dreams speak to us in our own language and in terms we already know. Occasionally, however, a dream figure will speak in a foreign tongue the dreamer doesn't understand, or she will experience a place, such as outer space, to which she has never been. These exceptions are powerful and meaningful, for they suggest that the dreamer is accessing deep levels of the collective unconscious that lie within, even though he or she is completely unaware of their existence. So, in some way, we are familiar with these dream events.

In *Creative Dreaming*, Patricia Garfield says that the "form of the god is predetermined (rather than being a recognition following the dream), that is, shaped by the expectations of the dreamer." She suggests, "As you formulate clearly your intended dream you will shape your future dream experience even more directly."

We know that dreams are closely connected to the intuitive sense and may arise from it. Sometimes a dreamer gets a dream-answer to a problem by deliberately inducing a dream, but at other times the answer arrives spontaneously. The technical term for this is *antecedent intuition*. Much of ordinary problem-solving, however difficult, is handled in this way. Remember the dream of Friedrich Kekulé, who discovered the molecular structure of benzene. His dream-answer was a supreme act of his intuition, which previously had been fed all the available facts and information relevant to the issue.

Here is an example from my own dream files of a dream of the antecedent intuitive type:

A few years ago I was working on an outline for a new book based on the planet Mercury. It was a complicated piece of work and at one point I got really stuck. For days I wrote and rewrote—and balled up the sheets and threw them in the trash basket. I couldn't understand what I had already written, let alone how to finish. In a state of utter frustration (which, by the way, is a necessary part of the intuitive process), I occupied myself with unrelated chores around the house. Then, a few nights later I had this dream.

I was in an art studio working with other people when the telephone rang. Someone answered it and said to me, "It's for you."

When I answered the dream phone, a rough, masculine voice said, "Hey, lady, we can't finish dis project until we get the artwork."

I was mystified and hadn't a clue what he was talking about.

"Who are you?" I questioned.

"Lady, dis is de Mercury Press and you better get that artwork down here pronto if you want this job finished."

"Where are you?" I asked.

"In the basement."

Like Kekulé, I awoke as if struck by lightning. Suddenly everything was clear to me. Immediately, I set to work to design the art, which was mythologically based. As I proceeded with this phase of the project, everything else fell into place—like magic.

What had happened was that although I had been working on the project for some time, and I knew that it would be illustrated, I had not yet integrated the art into the text. Even though I had chosen the artist and gathered and stored a lot of information relative to the drawings to be done, what I had neglected to do was to envision the project as a finished whole. It was this omission that had caused me to become blocked. And my dream friend came to the rescue in a most colorful manner, showing that my unconscious process was helping to solve the conscious problem.

Many Dream Explorers believe in "little people," a race of fairies or gnomes who emerge from hidden places to do the bidding of

Intuition without Antecedent

There's a type of intuition that requires no antecedent. It often works through your dreams. You are given information that you have not been seeking, you haven't been trying to solve a problem, and you aren't feeding your unconscious facts about the matter. It's rather like getting an unexpected e-mail that tells you something. This type of dream can be precognitive (predict the future), or it can be a message about an event that has already happened. For example, there have been many reports of people dreaming of an older relative who has just died without their knowledge. This sort of thing can also happen in an "altered" state, when the mind has slipped into the theta pattern described earlier. Therefore, it's always good to be alert to your dreams and daydreams for unexpected messages, which may be delivered by an unknown messenger.

humans. These beings are also known as *elementals*, or *nature spirits*, a term derived from the ancient concept that nature is animated by spirits—every tree, rock, stream, flower, bird, and animal has its own spirit, a belief held by Native Americans and other tribal peoples.

Robert Louis Stevenson's Brownies and my own rough-voiced basement worker seem to me to belong to this elemental dimension, and it is one to which you might pay close attention. When you acknowledge, respect, and align yourself with the elements of nature, you are given unexpected help because you are operating in harmony with natural forces.

> *Breezes at dawn have secrets to tell you.*
> *Don't go back to sleep.*
> *You must ask for what you truly want.*
> *Don't go back to sleep.*
> *People are going back and forth across the threshold*
> *Where the two worlds touch*
> *The door is round and open*
> *Don't go back to sleep.*
>
> RUMI, SUFI POET

Teen Dream Exercise

Dream Explorer Essay

Use this page to write a short essay on what you have just learned about Dream Explorers and the thoughts you have about this information. It's not a test; it's a way for you to remember the tips and clues gleaned from other cultures and to find ways to explore your own dreams successfully.

_____

_____

_____

_____

_____

_____

_____

_____

_____

_____

_____

_____

_____

_____

_____

_____

_____

_____

_____

_____

_____

_____

_____

_____

_____

_____

Teen Dream Exercise

How I Want to Use My Dreams

Based on what you have learned so far about what dreams can do for you and what they have done for others you have read about, make some general notes about what you'd like your future dreams to contribute to your life. See if you can remember a dream you've had that helped you deal with some real-life situation and write the dream in the blanks below. Also make notes of dreams you would like to experience.

_____

_____

_____

_____

_____

_____

_____

_____

_____

_____

_____

_____

_____

_____

_____

_____

_____

_____

_____

_____

_____

3

Interpretation of Dreams

"All dreams are given for the benefit of the individual, would he but interpret them correctly."

EDGAR CAYCE

Most dreams are full of images: of people dead and alive, known and unknown, animals both domestic and wild, landscapes and buildings familiar and strange, or any number of other symbolic images such as jewelry, household things, clothing, and so on. A dream usually has some kind of a story line. You may find yourself on an adventure of some kind. You may dream of celebrities or other famous people either from the present or the past.

I once had a fascinating dream of visiting the president Woodrow Wilson, who had been in office during the time of World War I, long before I was even born. During my dream visit to the president, we talked of many things of a psychic and occult nature. I wondered what it meant. When I discussed this dream with my dreamwork partner, who was a good bit older than I and very knowledgeable about matters concerning the occult, he told me that Woodrow Wilson had held seances in the White House! At the time, I was just beginning my own studies of the occult and having psychic experiences on a regular basis.

Food is another symbol that often appears in dreams. The kind of food and how it is presented and eaten (if eating occurs) are matters for the dreamer to understand. Food dreams may relate to what

you had for supper—or what you wanted to have and didn't get. Or you may have food concerns, such as being on a diet to lose weight or trying to gain weight.

The number of symbols that the dream-mind can produce is practically endless, and most of these symbols are up for individual interpretation. Some, however, have universal meaning. We'll discuss mostly the first kind in this chapter. We will take a look at some universal symbols in chapter 7 when we discuss creating your own dictionary of dream symbols.

Personal Dream Symbols

One of the best ways to get at the meaning of the symbols in your dreams is by *free association*. This is the method made popular by the psychologist Sigmund Freud. In this method, you simply go with the first thing that pops into your mind when the trigger word is given. Do the exercises presented on pages 48–50 in order to begin to get familiar with your own word associations.

Amplification of Symbolic Meanings

Once you have identified a symbol in a dream, you can use the free association process to get at its meaning. If you don't immediately get an associative thought about the dream symbol, work backward through your feelings and experiences with the symbol until you hit something that fits or makes sense. Suppose, for example, that you see a tiger in a dream. Do you like tigers or are they an object of fear? Maybe you saw a nature film recently about tigers and are concerned about their survival as a species. The important thing is to discover what a tiger means to you in the present, for the meanings of your symbols can change over time.

As you begin to work with your dreams on a regular basis and gain a high level of ability to recall your dreams (which we'll discuss in chapter 5), you will become familiar with your own personal symbolic style. Most of us are influenced symbolically by the objects we are familiar

with—such as religious symbols like crosses and pictures of saints or holy people—and also by our everyday life experiences. For example, if you have a pet of any kind, you are likely to dream about that animal. Of course, you may dream about animals even if you don't keep a pet, and you may dream about wild animals. But if you dream of your own pet, it will have personal significance to you alone.

Sometimes you have a dream that seems to complete some unfinished business of the day—say you had a math problem you couldn't solve and you dreamed yourself in a classroom with the solution written on the blackboard. Freud believed that dreams were "wish fulfillment" vehicles, and it is true that we can dream of things or experiences that we want (such as getting a date with a particular person) but dreams are much, much more than simple wish fulfillment. They are complex and multileveled, as you will realize by working steadily with your dreams.

Most dream symbols are not to be taken literally. You often need to do a bit of sleuthing to get at what the message of the dream symbol, or story, is for you. An example I read in one dream book was a dream of Bob Hope hopping on a pogo stick. At first, this seems nonsensical, but the dreamer was depressed and the dream was interpreted as "Hope springs eternal." Here's an example of a recent series of dreams of my own, concerning food.

"Then your I is no longer your mundane little self but the I of the Big Dreamer who is dreaming the whole universe."
Fred A. Wolf, Physicist

I was preparing to go on an eating program that required the elimination of all sugar, and as soon as I had set a date to begin I started having dreams of all kinds of luscious desserts—beautifully iced and decorated cakes, pies piled high with whipped cream, the most enticing confections of chocolate from cakes to cookies and everything in between, pastries stuffed with sweet cheese and iced with thick sugar, fancy French fruit tarts of every description.

At first, I took this to be simple resistance of my unconscious to changing my eating habits, but I actually don't eat a lot of sweets, and when I do have dessert I favor simple, homey things like custard, stewed fruit, or fruit cobbler.

I've never had a taste for heavily iced cakes, plus I am one of the few people on the planet who doesn't like chocolate! So why was I dreaming of all these fancy sweet foods that I wouldn't even want to eat?

My first take on the dreams—of which there were several during a week or so—was that I was feeling deprived in advance and that my imagination was plying me with these luscious images of sweets to weaken my decision to eliminate sweets. But this didn't make a lot of sense, as the fancy confections weren't what I'd want to eat anyway. So I looked deeper.

What was food as a symbol to me, especially this kind of elaborately prepared party food? Well, party food means a party—or at least company for dinner. I'd been going through a period of relative isolation, partly because I was busy writing and partly because I hadn't been feeling up to par. My social life had dropped to almost zero. The dreams were actually telling me that I was feeling deprived of—not the coming lack of sweets—but what special food, especially desserts, represents socially. Food of course represents nourishment; however, my dreams were not about nutrition! My first interpretation of deprivation was definitely a clue to the true meaning of the dreams. Yet they were a message that I needed, not sweets, but some sweet occasions and to take the time to be with people more. Can you think of a get-together that doesn't involve food? Usually fancy food, and always, desserts.

Using this as an example, think of what dreams of fancy desserts might mean to you. And if you've ever dreamed of food, try to remember what kind of food and under what circumstances you dreamed of it. Then think of what those various foods might symbolize for you.

Here's another example along the same lines, but with a different twist—that of a lemon peel!

A friend had been struggling with his weight, and he had decided to quit drinking his nightly martini in order to cut out some calories. He had decided to switch to a single glass of wine with dinner instead. He did this and found

himself enjoying his new way of dining. But then he started having dreams about martinis. For about a week, he told me, he had nothing but dreams featuring martinis, with a twist of lemon peel. He had always put olives in his martinis, not lemon peel, so this puzzled him. When he told me about the dreams, I flashed on the standard language of a bartender, who when taking an order for a martini will say, "Do you want a twist?" After some discussion of what the word twist meant to him, he revealed that he had recently twisted his ankle and it had been quite painful, but he hadn't bothered to see a doctor about the problem. His dream was showing him that a "twist" was in need of his attention. It didn't relate to his martini drinking at all, except that this was a familiar picture and dreams always speak in our own language, even if they do twist it around a bit!

Most dreams are not to be taken literally; just because you dream of someone dying does not mean the person will die. In fact, the literal interpretation of dreams can be dangerous and cause fear and anxiety. Also, dream books are not to be trusted. It's worth repeating that you have your own set of inner symbolic meanings. What a cat means to me—an avid cat lover—and what a cat means to someone who hates or fears cats would be something quite different. Always remember that your inner symbol-producing mechanism is yours alone, unique. That being emphasized, there are a few symbols that can be considered universal, such as the ocean or water representing the unconscious processes.

The best way for you to learn to interpret your own personal symbol system is by continually paying attention to your dreams, writing them down, and doing your own interpretations. Dream interpretation is an art, not a science, and no scientific sleep lab can read the content or measure the meaning of dreams. Isis, the ancient Egyptian goddess queen, was believed to say "No mortal has lifted my veil," and this can well apply to the scientific efforts to penetrate the mysteries of dream in sleep labs.

It is interesting to note that some types of dreams that we know to be quite common have never been reported from sleep labs (as least not as far as I have found in my research). One of these is the nightmare. It seems that people don't want to tell their deepest fears to a sleep lab researcher. Another common type is the wet dream, so named for when a male ejaculates semen while dreaming (though females also have this type of sexual dream). It is interesting to note that most of the subjects in sleep labs are young male college students, whom one might presume to often have wet dreams. But these are, apparently, considered too private to dream when under observation.

If you are just beginning to pay attention to your dreams, begin the process of interpretation by recording the symbols that appear most frequently. This applies especially to any recurring dreams or motifs you may experience. For example, I know that when my cat Fuzz (who's dead now) appears in a dream, it means my heart center is the subject of the dream. Depending on the story line of the dream and what Fuzz is doing or how we are interacting, I can figure out what the dream message about my heart is.

Recently, I dreamed that Fuzz had been hit by a car, but I knew instinctively that he was still alive. My brother was waiting outside in a car and I asked him to take me to find Fuzz and get an emergency vet. He did and Fuzz was saved. The dream came on the heels of a severe disappointment (one might say I was heartbroken), but I was being told that everything would come out all right in the end, which it did.

What is interesting about this dream is that even though I did not see the cat get hit by the car, I knew he was still alive. This told me that although I had been hurt emotionally, I would get over it. It also showed me that help was at hand—my brother was waiting in the car, and a vet was readily available. I had friends I could turn to who would help me to heal from a hurtful experience. In this way, our dreams spill over into everyday life.

"There are a lot of people on the planet right now who don't think that dreams are important. Perhaps it is that attitude which contributes to the ill health of the planet as a whole. If so, it depends more and more on you, the Spiritual Warriors of your generation, to weave the dreams that can heal the planet."

Dr. Laurel Ann Reinhardt,
"Dream Weaving," in
The Thundering Years
by Julie Johnson

The world of dream and intuition is really not divorced from our everyday reality, not a thing apart. Most people today think their dreams have nothing to do with real life, but they are wrong. We are all multifaceted beings with complexities of which often we are hardly aware. Too many people operate solely on linear thinking (the standard modern-day mode that is taught to young people in schools) and aren't aware that there are other ways to think and to obtain information. As Seth, the "spirit guide" that Jane Roberts "channeled" in a series of books "by" Seth, says, "You must change your ideas about dreaming, alter your concepts about it, before you can begin to explore it. Otherwise, your own waking prejudice will close the door."

All of the many facets of our personalities are operating all the time, even when we aren't conscious of them, just like our body chemistry goes on about its business when we are totally unaware of its functioning. Dreams can speak to parts of ourselves that we are ignoring, but we can't get the benefit from them unless we pay attention and approach their symbolic messages with an open mind and trusting heart.

While the symbolism in dreams may require interpretation, when we have difficulty with it we must realize that its purpose isn't to mystify us. As Dr. Jung says in his autobiography, *Memories, Dreams, Reflections*:

> I was never able to agree with Freud that the dream is a "façade" behind which its meaning lies hidden—a meaning already known but maliciously, so to speak, withheld from consciousness. To me dreams are a part of nature, which harbors no intentions to deceive but expresses something as best it can just as a plant grows or an animal seeks its food as best it can.

In working with your own personal dream symbols and motifs to decipher the meaning of your dreams, you may need to come at them from all angles. The following mind-mapping technique is especially helpful for those who function better using pictures and images, colors and drawings, than using a strictly verbal or writing mode.

As you practice interpreting your dreams and get more deeply into the process, it will become an enjoyable habit and you'll soon feel like an old pro at the game. You will get better and better, and your confidence will start to soar. Even if you have only a scrap of a dream to go on, it can lead to fruitful ideas. Here's an example from my personal files:

The Dream: A blond man speaks to me at a hotel of some sort. He breaks into French as his English fails him, and though I don't know French well I understand what he is saying. He gives me a key, which looks like the key to the security lock on my front door in real life. I ask what it is for and he replies that I will find out. When I go back to my room at the hotel I find that the key fits into a TV set, tuning it to a higher octave or a channel, like UHF, but much higher than that. I watch something on this "TV" but don't really understand it.

My interpretation of this brief fragment (for there was more I didn't remember) is that I am being given the "key" to a higher channel of myself. I don't yet know how to use this channel, and I can't understand what is being shown on this new type of TV. In other words, I am receiving communications in a language I don't fully understand. This dream had great meaning for me, as I was at that time in the process of becoming "psychic," but didn't really know what it meant or where it would lead. Later on, I experienced the "opening of the psychic door" on a trip to Germany, became a Tarot card reader, a professional astrologer, and a psychotherapist. This dream seemed to forecast these developments. That the man was blond suggests the Sun, or Higher Mind. His speaking in French might be a reference to my own French ancestors, all of whom spoke French as their native language, yet it was not taught to me so I grew up speaking English from day one. This hinted that I already "knew" the "foreign" language from hearing it spoken as a child.

With a little skill, you'll be able to start integrating your dreams into everyday life. We'll get into this in the next chapter, where we discuss how you can use dreams for specific purposes. However, please approach the entire subject of your dreams, their interpretations, and how you can use them with an open mind and in a relaxed state. Getting tense over interpretation is counterproductive and will block your efforts to make connections.

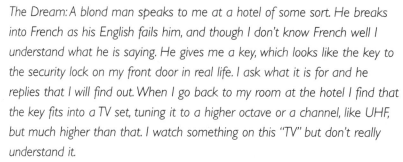

Teen Dream Exercise

Color Symbolism

Below is a list of common colors.
Jot down what they mean to you.

Blue _____

Green _____

Orange _____

Yellow _____

Turquoise _____

Red _____

Purple _____

Rose _____

Pink _____

Lavender _____

Indigo _____

Black _____

White _____

Gray _____

Brown _____

Teen Dream Exercise
Word Association

Here is a list of common terms that you probably encounter on a regular basis, either through personal experience or via TV or movies. In the blank space following each word, jot down what comes to you *immediately* as a meaning for that word. Don't pause to think; just take what comes. If nothing occurs to you right away, move on to the next word. Don't use any "dream dictionaries" to look up words—you are finding your own *personal* associations for these words that may act as symbols in your dreams.

Airplane _____	Dream _____	Ocean _____
Airport _____	Easter _____	Planet _____
Altar _____	Eating _____	Passing _____
Argument _____	Egg _____	Past _____
Artillery _____	Floor _____	Plenty _____
Automobile _____	Flowers _____	Pumpkin _____
Bacon _____	Flying _____	Purse _____
Ball _____	Food _____	River _____
Basement _____	Ghost _____	Rose _____
Beach _____	Grass _____	Sky _____
Boat _____	Green _____	Street _____
Book _____	Gun _____	Sugar _____
Bridge _____	Hat _____	Sun _____
Chair _____	House _____	Takeout _____
Child _____	Kiss _____	Telephone _____
Classroom _____	Knife _____	Television _____
Christmas _____	Lake _____	Train _____
Church _____	Leg _____	Tree _____
Computer _____	Letter _____	Walk _____
Crucifix _____	Mirror _____	Wallet _____
Demon _____	Mistake _____	Water _____
Desk _____	Money _____	Well _____
Doorway _____	Moon _____	Zoo _____

Teen Dream Exercise

Animal Symbols

Here is a list of common animals that you are probably familiar with, either through real-life experience or through books, movies, or TV. As you did in the Word Association exercise, jot down whatever comes immediately to mind in the blank following each animal's name. If nothing comes immediately, move on to the next word. Once again, don't use any commercial "dream dictionaries." The idea is to connect with your own personal associations for these animal names, which may act as symbols in your dreams.

Alligator _____	Fish _____	Rabbit _____
Ant _____	Fly _____	Raccoon _____
Antelope _____	Fox _____	Rat _____
Bat _____	Frog _____	Raven _____
Bear _____	Gerbil _____	Salamander _____
Bird _____	Gorilla _____	Seagull _____
Bull _____	Guinea pig _____	Seahorse _____
Bug _____	Hawk _____	Shark _____
Butterfly _____	Horse _____	Skunk _____
Cat _____	Hummingbird _____	Snake _____
Caterpillar _____	Kitten _____	Spider _____
Chicken _____	Lion _____	Squirrel _____
Cougar _____	Lioness _____	Swan _____
Cow _____	Lizard _____	Tiger _____
Coyote _____	Monkey _____	Toad _____
Deer _____	Moth _____	Turkey _____
Dog _____	Mouse _____	Turtle _____
Dolphin _____	Opossum _____	Weevil _____
Dragonfly _____	Otter _____	Whale _____
Duck _____	Owl _____	Wolf _____
Eagle _____	Peacock _____	Wolverine _____
Egret _____	Porcupine _____	Worm _____
Elk _____	Porpoise _____	Zebra _____

Teen Dream Exercise

Mind-Mapping Technique

To do the mind-mapping technique, you will need a large sheet of paper and some colored markers, paints, crayons, colored pencils, and so forth, some quiet time, and a space where you will be undisturbed. The purpose is to connect your dream symbols to your inner meanings. This exercise involves a method known as *clustering*.

To make a cluster drawing, first draw a circle (or any other shape) in the center of the page. Start with a general theme using a word or a picture from your dream and write this in the center, using any color you feel drawn to. Try not to think or analyze as you go along. This is a right-brain exercise; just follow the inner flow. Draw straight lines out from the center circle and make more circles (or shapes), and fill those in with whatever comes to you, or with other symbols from the dream that seem to relate. Continue choosing words and group them in little clusters out from the center, again in whatever colors seem to "call" to you. Just let the drawing process flow and make connections until you feel you have finished. There's no minimum and no maximum. Choose as many or as few words as you like and arrange them spontaneously. Afterward, pay attention to the colors you chose and see what feeling tones the colors suggest, based on your reaction to the color list in the previous exercise.

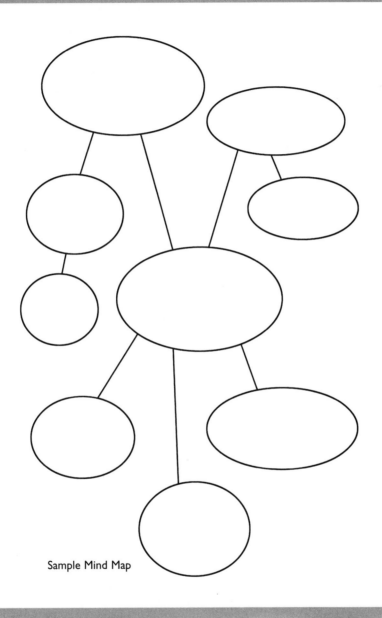

Sample Mind Map

Teen Dream Exercise

Dream Interpretation Using the Tarot

For those of you who use the Tarot cards or are interested in beginning to use them, you may find them helpful in doing dream interpretations. You can use a simple layout or a more complex one. (See my book *Tarot for Teens* for more information.) The following is a simple method to get you started.

While concentrating on your dream, shuffle or mix your deck of cards. You can use the Major Arcana only or the entire deck. Lay out a line of seven cards face down, with Card I on the left and Card 7 at the far right, and turn each card face up in that order. Here's what the card positions indicate.

Card I: This position gives a general overview of the dream.

Card 2: This position is an indication of what type of dream you are asking about—whether its nature is psychological, precognitive, guidance, or something else.

Card 3: This position reveals the core content of the dream message.

Card 4: This position enlarges on the dream message, is more specific.

Card 5: This position suggests the relationship of the dream to real life.

Card 6: This position indicates what action to take to incorporate the dream into your waking life.

Card 7: This position is the synthesis card that pulls it all together. It can be considered the outcome card.

If you draw one of the court cards—king, queen, knight, page—then you need to find out what person the card represents in your life. Here's a list of possible people who might appear in your dream and be represented by a court card figure. Go over the list and write down next to each word what that person means to you symbolically (even if you don't know such a person or have one in your life at this time).

Mother _____

Father _____

Grandmother _____

Grandfather _____

Aunt _____

Uncle _____

Brother _____

Sister _____

Cousin _____

Teacher _____

Priest _____

Pastor _____

Law Officer _____

Judge _____

Politician _____

Doctor _____

Boss _____

Lawyer _____

Principal _____

Senator _____

If for any reason you don't understand a card or you feel confused by it or don't think it applies, just draw another card at random to illuminate the first card. You can draw as many clarification cards at random as you like until you get a feeling about the meaning of your dream.

On the Non-Interpretation of Dreams

Not every dream has to be interpreted. While it is true that dream interpretation is a valuable thing to do on a regular basis, it is also true that it's not needed for every single dream you have. Some dreams can simply be enjoyed—such as dreams of flying or of taking trips to outer space. You might attend a fun party in a dream—and while you might have just attended a party or might have one in your near future, you don't necessarily have to dig deeply for meaning. It's always good to be aware of your dreams for messages of importance, but it's not good to become obsessive about understanding the "meaning" of every dream you have. This is not a college course or an exam, it's just part of your life. So, take it as it comes. Interpret when the dream seems to need interpretation, but don't worry or sweat it if you either don't want to try interpreting or if you feel the dream is complete in itself as an experience without interpretation.

Always remember that you are an explorer who is tracking through unknown territory without a map. Be willing to take chances and to encounter strange experiences and foreign or unusual situations. Remember, there's nothing in any dream—including a nightmare—that can actually hurt you. You can, and always will, wake up to your ordinary life. However, by paying attention to your dreams, you will wake up to a world full of meaning that is greatly enriched.

Dreams and Everyday Life

Why should we investigate dreams? Of what use are they to us in our everyday lives? Can something that isn't "real" actually be of help to us as we go about our daily activities, facing problems, dealing with the many facets of our lives?

The answer is a definite *yes*. Not only have many cultures over the centuries believed that dreams have significance, as we saw in chapter 2, but now some scientists in our own culture believe that dreams do indeed affect our lives, and vice versa.

For example, the psychologist Leonard Handler, in an article in the journal *Psychotherapy: Theory, Research, and Practice* entitled "The Amelioration of Nightmares in Children," tells the story of an eleven-year-old boy named Johnny who was tortured by frequent nightmares. He had a recurring nightmare in which a terrifying monster would chase him. Sometimes the monster caught Johnny and hurt him. Over a period of eighteen months, two or three times a week, Johnny would wake up screaming and run to his parents' bedroom for comfort. He could not fall asleep without a nightlight. Finally, Johnny's parents consulted Dr. Handler, who assured Johnny that he could help him, that together they would get rid of the horrible, frightening monster. After a few sessions during which Johnny came to trust him, the doctor sat Johnny on his knee and encircled him with a fatherly arm. He told the boy that he would protect him from the monster and then asked him to close his eyes and imagine the monster there in the room with them. Although he was scared, Johnny agreed to cooperate and,

Dream Power

"We can deal with our problems at their origin in our own minds. We can learn about ourselves and grow. We can unify our personalities. We can transform our fear-producing dream enemies into dream friends. It is true. We can build into our dream world friendly images that will help us not only in our dreams but in our waking life as well. We can make dream friends who will provide us with solutions to our problems and with marvelous creative products. Dream friends can show us how to solve a knotty problem . . . sing a new song. . . . Whatever our problems are, dreams can provide novel ideas and sometimes magnificent resolutions."

Patricia Garfield,
Creative Dreaming

shutting his eyes tight, showed the doctor by a prearranged signal that the monster was there with them.

Holding Johnny close, Handler banged his hand on the desk loudly and shouted over and over, "Get out of here, you lousy monster, leave my friend John alone!" As Johnny quivered in the doctor's arms, Handler continued shouting and banging. "Get away and stay away! Don't you ever come back or I'm going to get you!"

After quite a few minutes of this performance, Johnny joined in the effort to get rid of the monster, pounding his own small hand on the desk with the doctor's and shouting at the top of his voice, "Get away and leave me alone!" Then Dr. Handler turned out the lights, and although Johnny was startled to be in the dark, soon he was again yelling at the monster to go away and leave him alone—or else!

They continued this procedure throughout the session, and when Johnny left his office Handler told him that if he saw the monster again he was to do exactly the same thing. At the next week's appointment, Handler asked if Johnny had seen the monster again. He had, but the boy had followed instructions and yelled at it. It vanished. Once again, Johnny and Handler practiced monster-scaring. After that, during a six-month period, Johnny had only two nightmares—neither one about the monster, who had departed for good. Although most of us aren't troubled by such severe nightmares, this is a good example of how waking life can influence dreams.

Your dreams can be affected by many things: what you ate for supper, or even lunch or breakfast; what images you put into your mind—from TV or video or conversation, especially arguments—before bedtime; problems you are facing; your relationships with parents, other relatives, friends, and love interests; your hopes and aspirations; your basic beliefs; communications during the day or recent past; long past events from your childhood; plans for the future, such as going away to college or getting a job; and a host of other things.

But how about dreams influencing waking life? How does this mysterious process interact with what we do when we are awake?

Although no one can say for certain *what* dreams are, *where* they come from, or even *why* we have them, there's no doubt that they are important to the quality of our lives. Even people who claim not to dream (they just don't remember their dreams) are in some subtle way affected by their dreams, if only as an unexplainable shift in mood. Anyone who has studied their own dreams closely or has studied dreams professionally, as I have as a psychotherapist, knows that dreams and waking life are intimately interconnected.

Dreams are of many sorts and are many layered. Some are simple, with messages for daily life that are easy to interpret if you try. Some are complex and require more attention. And, yes, some defy interpretation. That does not mean they are unimportant or that they don't affect us deeply. There is a lot in this world that humans don't understand. Much about the human mind, psyche, memory, and potential remains a mystery to us despite our persevering efforts to penetrate the mystery.

So, your mission, should you decide to accept it, is to do your own dream research. Sleep labs at universities and in other institutional settings notwithstanding, the best sleep lab is your own bed, or wherever you happen to sleep or nap. You are the best interpreter of your dreams. You can get clues and guidance from dream books such as this one (though you can never trust those "cookie cutter" dream dictionaries to say what anything means for sure), but by far the best tool for understanding how your dreams connect up with your everyday life is your own attention to them.

USING DREAMS FOR SPECIFIC PURPOSES

One of the most interesting aspects of dreams is their potential to be put to use for specific purposes. The rest of this chapter is going to deal with this subject. Of course, it's impossible to cover every situation a dream can throw light on or every problem dreams can help solve. But this chapter will give you an overview of how you can use dreams for specific purposes, along with tips to make it easier.

"Dreaming provides a time and a space for personally carrying out our own future development as awakened individuals."

P. Erik Craig,
Director of the Center for
Existential Studies

Sequential Relaxation Technique

Lie comfortably on the floor or on a bed and breathe deeply several times, consciously inhaling fresh energy and consciously exhaling all negative tension. Then, starting with your toes, focus on each part of your body in turn: feet, ankles, calves, knees, thighs, hips, lower back, upper back, abdomen, chest, arms, hands, neck, spine, head. As you focus on each part, mentally instruct it to relax completely and linger there until you feel the muscles loosen. Tell each set of muscles to go limp and feel yourself gradually sinking into an inert state of being. When you have finished with this sequence, do it again, but this time begin with your head and move to your toes.

How to Incubate a Specific Dream

Before you request a specific dream, be sure to relax your mind and body completely. You can use the sequential relaxation technique offered here or repeat your own relaxation affirmations.

Step 1: Decide in advance what you want to dream, what you want the dream to resolve, or what question you want answered.

Step 2: Write your desired dream or question on a piece of paper. Be as specific as you can, but don't ask about silly or trivial matters, such as what dress to wear to a party or if so-and-so likes you.

Step 3: Put the paper under your pillow or near your bed.

Step 4: Tell yourself with conviction that you will have the dream you want.

Step 5: Believe that you can trust yourself to dream the dream you ask for.

Step 6: Be prepared to write down the dream when you wake up.

Step 7: Be open to whatever comes to you in your dream, and work with it.

Step 8: Tell yourself you will remember the dream in detail.

Step 9: Be willing to experiment and try again if necessary.

THE HEALING POWER OF DREAMS

In his book *Meaning and Medicine,* Larry Dossey, M.D., says, "One of the most significant possible breakthroughs in understanding how healing comes about is the realization that we all possess an inner source of healing and strength that operates behind the scenes with no help whatsoever from our conscious mind." I call this source our "secret helper," and it is most often revealed to us through dreams.

We have already noted that people in many cultures have used dreams as the basis for healing. In the Greek temples of healing, the god or goddess was invoked through carefully induced dreaming. Native American medicine men and medicine women may have been the first doctors, as they used dreams to promote healing by contacting supernatural "spirits" who had the power to cure illness.

Modern Shamans

Today, we have a new breed of shamans—men and women who have studied the ancient practices. Many of these people are born, raised, and educated in Western cultures. They have come to be shamans either through accidentally crossing the path of a shaman teacher or by actively seeking out these elders who know the old ways and are willing to teach them.

These modern shamans are bringing into our culture some of the dream wisdom that we need to balance our way of life and to stop destroying our world. One such person is John Perkins, who has studied extensively with the Shuar Indians of South America and written books about his experiences. He describes a shaman as a "man or woman who journeys into Dreamtime or parallel worlds and uses the subconscious, along with physical reality, to effect change."

Perkins's first experience with shamans came when he worked in the Peace Corps in the Amazon rain forest during the late 1960s. Then, after a career as a business executive he left the business world to seek training in Ecuador by native shamans. He began to take groups of people into the rain forest for seminars and workshops with the Shuar people on "ecotourist" tours.

As Perkins explains in his book *The World Is As You Dream It: Shamanic Teachings from the Amazon and Andes,* dreaming is at the heart of the Shuar culture, and their philosophy is that the world is created through our dreams.

"If the world is as we dream it, then every reality is a matter of perception. . . . When we give our energy to a different world, the world is transformed."

John Perkins,
The World Is As You Dream It

Journeying to Other Realms

"In the countless exhilarating hours of assisting various indigenous shamans in healing ceremonies, I learned rituals and tools to help focus and direct energy. As I spent more and more time at the homes of these shamans, I learned that journeying is not only an essential practice of shamanic work, but an integral part of life in shamanic communities. It is encouraged, discussed at length within the extended family and community every day, and allowed to develop into a way of life. This way of being creates other realms in which to learn and grow, other realms in which to play and rehearse, other realms in which to live. These other realms and life experiences are not thought of as any less real or useful than the life and realm that we all commonly experience."

Eve Bruce,
Shaman, M.D.

The first rule in using dreams for healing is—as always—to take them seriously. While some psychotherapists use dream interpretation as part of their treatment method, few in the medical profession have paid any attention to the healing power of dreams. It is up to the individual to heed the messages coming from the unconscious.

This is particularly important for teenagers, whose complaints about health—mental and physical—often are not taken seriously enough, or who are shuffled off to a doctor who hasn't a clue about the real issues involved. This doctor may be a person who either intimidates youngsters or simply treats them as adults, without giving special attention to the needs and problems of teens. So you can help yourself considerably by using your own dreams for healing.

Here is a quite dramatic example of a healing dream I had in the wake of a major problem.

After working for weeks to draft material for a new book on a topic close to my heart, I received a lukewarm response from the editor who previously had shown enthusiastic interest in the project. She suggested extensive changes that distorted my original intention, and against my better judgment, I tried to do what she wanted. It was a serious mistake. In my eagerness to have the book published, I failed to notice that I broke one of my own personal commandments: Be true to yourself. Undermining my personal integrity by trying to please someone who didn't understand the fundamental concept at the heart of the book cost me dearly.

The first symptom was the usual one for me: a sore throat. Instinct told me I was in trouble, and I immediately took preventive measures to stave off what I call an "emotional flu." Too late. The emotional and psychological damage was done and was translated into my body—the piper was calling to be paid, and I got very sick.

For two weeks I lay in bed, coughing my head off day and night while I worried about not getting the revised manuscript finished on schedule. Then, during a feverish dream I heard a voice say, "If it's going to make you sick, don't do it!" I determined that I would return to my basic principles of integrity and drop the project—but I was still very ill.

In the third week of my suffering, as I lay there utterly exhausted by the long bouts of coughing and the crushing ache my body had become, I dreamed of a wolf, lying sick and alone on the forest floor on a pile of dead leaves. Wolves are social animals who live in packs; that's why the saying "a lone wolf" indicates someone unusual. The sick wolf of my dream had nothing to help him get well except his inner wolf nature. His only course was to follow his deep instinctual knowledge of what would bring him back to health.

When I first saw him, he appeared to be unconscious. The sight of his limp, inert body with the glowing eyes filmed over brought a rush of compassion and love for him, and I desperately wanted to do something to help him. As I stood over his prostrate body, wishing I were a veterinarian, something magical happened: I became the wolf. And, as the wolf, I understood profoundly the meaning of integrity. In the human world, the word integrity has come to mean something like honesty, but what it really means is wholeness. What possesses integrity has never been compromised: it is in a state of completeness, undivided, unbroken. Though grievously ill, the wolf was in total possession of his integrity. He was, most deeply, exactly who he was, absolutely true to his fundamental nature. He wasn't trying to please anyone. He simply was.

Joseph Campbell says that "myth is metaphor." I was not just dreaming about a wolf—I was the wolf! And, as the wolf, I lay there on the floor of the forest primeval and called up from within my wolf-self those most basic instinctive animal powers that sustain us automatically, when we allow ourselves to be in touch with them. Dreams are the perfect medium for making this vital contact with our deepest selves.

After this dream, I slept for many hours, the first healing sleep I'd had in the weeks of my illness. I awoke feeling refreshed, clear-headed, and buoyant, as if I had been reborn. A vivid memory remained of actually being the wolf, a living creature with no one but Nature to call upon for healing. If you had asked me to pick an animal to be, I'd choose a tiger or a dolphin. But the wolf-self was such a profound experience that I realized I had contacted my inner self in animal form. From this dream I not only received the healing I needed for my sick body, I also gained an important insight into my own inner workings and the necessity of maintaining my personal integrity—as well as the danger of violating it.

Teen Dream Exercise

Have a Healing Dream

Following the steps given earlier in this chapter for incubating a dream, make an attempt to have a healing dream. Use the spaces provided here to write your dream experience. Notice how your body felt before you went to sleep and how it felt when you woke up. Note what images were in your mind as you fell asleep and what symbols appeared in your dream. Were there people, animals, objects? If you succeeded, did the dream fulfill your request? Try your hand at interpreting your dream, and judge how it helped you. Whether the healing you seek is physical, emotional, or spiritual, as you improve you'll begin to realize how powerful an ally your dreams are, and that your body, mind, and spirit have the capacity to heal you.

Relaxation technique I used:

_____

_____

Results:

_____

_____

How my body felt:

_____

_____

_____

How I phrased my dream request:

_____

_____

The dream I had:

_____

_____

_____

_____

My dream symbols:

_____

_____

How I felt when I woke up:

_____

_____

How I felt about the dream:

_____

_____

Things I liked about the dream:

_____

_____

Things I did not like about the dream:

_____

_____

Things I would change next time:

_____

_____

Healing Dream Messages

Sometimes a dream with a healing message will come along by itself, unasked for. A friend who practices hands-on healing therapy related the following dream to me:

I am working on a young man, an AIDS patient. I want so much to help him, but I know there is only so much I can do. Suddenly I see myself covered with the dark spots of the Kaposi's cancer. Thinking I have caught it from him, I step back in horror and begin frantically to try to peel the scabs from my body. I wake up shaken and tearful.

This woman had devoted herself to treating AIDS patients and was utterly exhausted from the efforts she was making. She already suffered from a weakened heart, but instead of taking the prescribed rest, she insisted on continuing her work, saying, "My patients need me." I warned her about the risks to her health and begged her to take a vacation, but she insisted on overextending herself . . . until she had this dream. Finally, she understood the harm she was doing to her own health in her efforts to heal others, and she recognized the dangers to herself of her selfless attitude. The dream vividly showed how her compulsion to "aid" was harming her. The dream acted as a warning device, forcing her to acknowledge what she was ignoring.

From my personal files I can pull another example of an unexpected healing dream. I was feeling fatigued and under par. I couldn't identify anything specific that was wrong, but one night I had a brief dream in which a doctor in the standard white coat said to me clearly: "Take vitamin C." That was it. The next day I doubled up on my regular intake of vitamin C and in a few days felt fine again. Obviously, my body was suffering from a vitamin deficiency that was not enough to make me sick but was sufficient to lower my vitality. No regular, real M.D. would have picked up on something so subtle, but my "inner doctor" knew just what the problem was and told me about it, point blank.

Dream Up the Life You Want

Your dreams can give first-rate help in many other areas of life. Creativity is a major one. Chapter 1 told about some famous artists and scientists who solved problems or got ideas through their dreams. You can do this too. You can use your dreams to help you with difficult schoolwork or in preparing for an exam or a sporting event. And you can put dreams to use in relationships of all kinds: with your parents, brothers and sisters, relatives, teachers, and—of course—with your love interests.

The writer Ardath Mayhar, who has published forty books of science fiction, mystery, fantasy, and westerns, told me that when she was really going with a book she usually dreamed about the next day's work, seeing the scenes she would write the next day. She also said that she had gotten many of her ideas for her fantasy and science fiction books from her dreams.

A writers' group I belong to reports similar experiences. One member says, "I often find myself in a library and my book is published and sitting on the shelf. I pick up my own book and read a few pages and—though I don't remember what I read when I wake up—the words just flow the next day with no effort." Another writer comments that whenever he feels "blocked," he takes a nap, after which—even if he didn't ask for or even remember a dream—the block vanishes. I've had this napping experience myself, so I suppose it's common. You might try taking naps when you are trying to solve a creative problem.

You don't have to be a writer or an artist to get creative ideas or to incubate dreams for specific purposes. In her book *Creative Dreaming*, Patricia Garfield makes this point by saying, "Ordinary dreamers are able to train themselves to have creative dreams in the area of their [interest]."

Teen Dream Tip

Dreams you dream when asleep at different times of day will have different qualities. Experiment with this by taking naps at odd hours, like before dinner, or whenever you get the chance on holidays, vacations, and weekends, when you don't have to be woken up by an alarm clock for school. Keep notes.

Teen Dream Exercise

Using Your Dreams to Improve Your Life

The following group of exercises will lead you toward incubating dreams for the purposes that interest you. These are only guidelines. You can use them as a jumping-off point for your own set of reasons to use your dreams. Consider them as "brainstorming" to identify areas of your life that you want help with. When you are clear on just how you want your dreams to assist you, you'll then know how to word your requests to your dream mind.

SCHOOLWORK

I want to make the following changes in my schoolwork:

Attitude_____

Grades_____

Approach_____

Consistency_____

Habits_____

PHYSICAL SELF AND GENERAL WELL-BEING

I want to make the following changes in my physical self:

My appearance

_____

_____

My attitude/feelings about my appearance

_____

_____

My self-image

_____

_____

My health _____

My weight _____

My eating habits _____

My clothing _____

Exercise _____

I have a chronic problem with _____

Extracurricular activities, sports, job

I want to make the following changes in my life:

Social events _____

Membership in clubs or organizations _____

Volunteer activities _____

Sports activities _____

Outside lessons _____

Job/work _____

Relationships

I want to make the following changes in my relationships:

Mother _____

Father _____

Stepmother _____

Stepfather _____

Siblings _____

Other relatives _____

Friends _____

Boyfriend/girlfriend_____

_____

Sexual activity _____

_____

Write a short essay describing the following: the nature of your relationships in general; what you feel good about in a relationship; what you feel bad about in a relationship; the pattern of your intimate relationships; the pattern of your relationship with your parents; the pattern of your relationship with brothers and sisters; what makes you happiest in any relationship; what you think an ideal relationship would be like.

_____

_____

_____

_____

_____

_____

_____

_____

_____

_____

_____

_____

_____

_____

SPIRITUAL LIFE

I want to examine my spiritual life in the following ways:

What I believe in now_____

_____

What I was brought up to believe in_____

I would like to develop spiritually along these lines_____

_____

How I feel about my spiritual life _____

I would be more spiritual if I _____

_____

I would like to change/experience _____

_____

GUIDANCE

I would like to receive guidance on:

1._____

2._____

3._____

4._____

5._____

6._____

7._____

8._____

HOPES AND WISHES

This month I would like to _____

_____

_____

Next month I would like to _____

_____

_____

Within six months I would like to _____

_____

_____

Over the coming year I would like to _____

_____

After high school I'd like to _____

_____

In college I want to study _____

_____

How I envision myself in five years _____

_____

_____

What I'd like to accomplish with my life _____

_____

_____

_____

Guidelines for Using Dreams for Specific Purposes

- Learn to eliminate fear-producing dream images by willing yourself to overcome them in the dream state.

- Activate your creative dream faculty by filling yourself with images of the rich variety in the real world. Read, look at art, listen to music, study what interests you in addition to regular school assignments, look at nature magazines and films. Take nature walks and observe what you see closely, especially animal life. Remember that your unconscious records everything you experience and feel.

- For school-related or other topics, prepare by filling yourself with information. Do Internet searches and read books on the topic. The more involved you are with a subject, especially one that involves you emotionally, the more help you will get when you call upon your dream-mind for assistance.

- Program yourself to produce creative solutions to problems of all sorts—from the small to the large. When you achieve a solution to a small problem, you are strengthening your "dream muscles" for more difficult questions.

- Give yourself specific dream assignments. Ask for a dream to resolve a particular issue and then work with what you produce. Dream first—evaluate later. Accept that all the elements you need are within you, in your existing body of knowledge.

- Be patient with your process. Persist in asking, dreaming, and working with the symbols from your dreams. Develop positive symbols and invite helpful dream figures.

- Give special attention to recurring dreams. They are messages about what is going on in your psyche and what is asking for your conscious attention.

Problem Solving with Dreams

The ability to devise creative products and solutions to problems advances as you draw upon your dream life and develop skills both in dreaming and in interpreting dreams. As you consciously pay attention to your dreams and use your dream symbols regularly, you'll soon be an expert at getting the information and help you need.

The Super Power of Dreams

In 1996, the actor Christopher Reeve, famous for his movie portrayal of Superman, was thrown from his horse during a jumping competition. The injury he suffered resulted in paralysis from the neck down. Prior to his accident, the six-foot-four Reeve had been extremely athletic—swimming, sailing, parasailing, horseback riding, and so on. Being unable to use his body after such an active life must have been extremely traumatic to him. However, his mind was alert and unharmed, as was his indomitable spirit. Reeve determined that, one day, he *would* walk again. He never gave up hope, although he could not move a single muscle. With the aid of physical therapists and the support of his wife and children, Reeve kept up a program of exercises. To the amazement of his doctors, one day he was able to move his index finger. Other improvements followed—small, but still amazing, like a miracle.

Reeve was interviewed on the PBS radio program *Fresh Air* on September 30, 2001. During the discussion, the interviewer asked Reeve if he dreamed of himself as disabled. His answer was, "No. I always dream of myself being athletic and active." Asked what his doctors thought of this, he replied that they had told him that his dreams of himself being physically as he was prior to the injury had opened new neural pathways in his brain, and, in their opinion, this was what caused him to make such astonishing progress. In spinal injuries of this magnitude, there is usually no hope at all, and so the tiniest bit of voluntary movement—the brain directing the muscles to move, which most of us take for granted, was almost miraculous.

No doubt Reeve's absolute conviction that he would walk again was a powerful influence on his dreams, which rallied inner forces to help him. He still has a long way to go, but he has reason for his hope and powerful reinforcement from his dream life that he will indeed walk again. This illustrates perfectly the super power of dreams.

As the true story about Christopher Reeve demonstrates, dreams have strong potential for affecting our lives, even in recovery from severe injuries. How this actually works is a subject that science has barely studied. But you don't have to wait until scientists prove the value of dreams before you can start using your own productively. In fact, you can start tonight.

Dream Recall

So far, you've learned about what dreams can do for you, about ancient and native peoples' longtime use of dreams for various purposes, how to start interpreting your dreams, and how to incubate your own dreams for specific purposes. In this chapter, you are going to learn how to *remember* your dreams.

Although there is no scientific proof that recalling our dreams makes them any more effective, it does seem that in general when we pay attention to things, we are more effective. Christopher Reevesaid that his dreams of being his old athletic self were vivid and that he remembered and enjoyed them. Recall that the proverb says, "An unremembered dream is like an unopened letter from God." This doesn't mean that dreams you don't remember are useless. No doubt they do their work anyway, but certainly recalling your dreams and working with them can only be a plus. At the very least, you'll get valuable information—and fabulous entertainment at times.

Dream recall is a funny thing. Some dreams fade away upon awakening no matter how hard we try to remember; others are so vivid that we couldn't forget them if we tried. (I still remember some dreams I had as a teenager, many years ago.) There are so many variables involved in what is an extremely complex process—and we don't know the half of them. For example, drugs can have a powerful effect on dreams. The Native Americans and other native cultures, especially in South America, regularly used certain plant substances (such as peyote and "magic" mushrooms) to induce desired dreams. I don't advise using drugs, but if you are taking a legal prescription drug it might be affecting your dreams. Alcohol, too, can have an effect on dreams, especially if consumed in large quantities. And I suspect that many other substances—what we eat, drink, touch, breathe—also have their effects. Girls may find that their dreams and dream recall are affected by where they are in their menstrual cycle. The phases of the Moon may also be a factor in dreaming, especially for girls. (See "The Moon" further on in the chapter.) That's why I continue to say, "Be a Dream Explorer." And keep records. (In chapter 6 we'll discuss keeping a Dream Diary and you'll do some exercises to help you recall your dreams and daytime circumstances before you sleep.)

Of course, even the most careful and dedicated dreamers don't remember every single dream. I've been practicing dreamwork for many years and there are still times when I wake up and remember only one or two dreams, or even none at all. There's no right and wrong about dream recall. Some people might by nature be more tuned in to their dreams than others. Usually, it's the extrovert, the outward-oriented person, who doesn't remember dreams much, while the introvert, or inward-turned person, remembers them more easily. No matter which type you are, though, you can increase your ability. The key is to train yourself on a consistent basis, using the steps in this chapter. It's not really difficult to learn to remember dreams regularly, almost every day/night cycle. But don't beat up on yourself when you don't.

Some dreams are so vivid and even startling that they wake us up in the middle of the night. When that happens, the message is really important. It's a good idea to keep a pad and pen or pencil by your bed—or even a tape recorder. A pen with a small light is an excellent tool, as you don't have to scribble notes in the dark that may be illegible in the morning. As you work with recalling and recording your dreams, you'll discover the method that is best for you. We are all different and need to find our own ways of doing things.

Teen Dream Tip

Attitude is everything. Valuing your dream product is the first step to remembering it. Always give your dream a title, and date it. This is important. Giving a title to a dream makes it special.

Teen Dream Tip

One popular method for dream recall that's been around a long time and seems to work is to tell yourself before you fall asleep, "I will remember my dreams in detail" and then to immediately drink half a glass of water. When you wake up, drink the other half. Try it and see if it works for you.

INCREASING YOUR DREAM MEMORY

The best time to remember dreams is when you awaken spontaneously, not by an alarm clock, radio, or outside noise. When you wake up naturally, it is always at the end of a REM, or dream, period. Also, the last dream of the night is the longest and most vivid, thus giving you more to hold on to when you wake up.

Even if you have remembered a dream, often in the press of the morning's routine—usually rushed for teens and their families—a fog may cloud your memories of the night's dreaming. You know you have to get up, dress, gather your things, get to school or sports practice, and if those activities are uppermost in your mind your dreams may fade away. You may retain the general flavor or color of the dream but lose the rest. This is why it's a good idea to concentrate on dream recall during the times when you can wake up naturally and when the atmosphere isn't pressured or hurried—in other words, on weekends, holidays, and vacations, when you have more leisure to lie in bed and remember your dreams. While being sick isn't fun, it *is* another good time to practice dream recall, because you are usually alone and in bed for hours at a time.

Still, you can practice dream recall on school nights too. I find that clients who begin the process of remembering their dreams become so fascinated and rewarded that they find ways to wake up naturally amid busy lives. One of these ways is to set your "internal alarm clock," which isn't hard to learn to do. With a bit of practice, you can program yourself to wake up without the alarm so that you are not catapulted out of a sound, dreaming sleep by the raucous noise of a mechanical device. It's easier on your nervous system too! Even if you have to use an alarm clock, you can set it a few minutes early and press the snooze button for a bit of quiet time to catch those sometimes elusive dreams before they vanish.

Once you're awake, lie still with your eyes closed and review your dreams. If at first you don't remember anything, continue to relax quietly until you recover a feeling about a dream or get some images. Usually there is a story, and sometimes the plot will follow as you think about the images and what they mean to you. Jot down whatever you remember, no matter how fragmentary. You will get better and better at this in time. Even fragments collected over time can function like pieces of a jigsaw puzzle to form a complete picture. Also practice remembering during the day by going over your notes. Often, the whole dream is still lying there just below consciousness and can be brought to mind.

KEYS TO DREAM RECALL

First, pay attention.

Second, expect positive results.

Third, accept what you produce.

Fourth, use your imagination to interpret the symbols in your dreams.

Fifth, be curious about your entire dream world and eager to explore its territory.

Sixth, have a definite purpose when you want a dream to serve you, and concentrate on the subject about which you want dream help.

Seventh, be filled with gratitude that you have this wonderful opportunity to explore your inner world anytime you sleep. Like Aladdin's cave, it is filled with treasure.

In addition to these seven steps, there is a crucial factor in being able to recall dreams fully, frequently, and easily: the desire to do so. If you really want to remember your dreams, you will. This may sound too simple, and yes, it takes practice, but like anything else you want very badly you will find a way to make it happen. Often, once you

Attention!

Remember that attention is the first key to dream recall. Paying attention to details increases both their volume and their vividness. Watch for anything that seems to have particular meaning or significance—a particular word, place, object, number, color—especially as symbols tend to be repeated. Often you can follow a familiar symbol and get back the whole dream. As you become accustomed to this process, you may find yourself spontaneously recalling portions of the night's dreams during the day. When this happens, write them down just as soon as you can.

Dream Tea

Many herbs are used for promoting sleep. The Celestial Seasonings brand has a blend called "Sleepytime" that I have found soothing and restful as a nighttime drink. It contains chamomile, spearmint (which settles the stomach), lemon grass, tilia flowers, blackberry leaves, orange blossoms, hawthorn berries, and rosebuds. Other herbs you can use to brew dream teas are hops, mugwort, and rosemary, usually available at health food stores in bulk. You can also try out other herbal tea blends already in tea bags.

Easy-Sleep Tea

To make a cup of Easy-Sleep Tea, you'll need 1/2 teaspoon of licorice and 1/2 teaspoon of dried mullein. Put a cup of cool water in a pan with the herbs, bring to a boil, remove from heat, cover, and let cool. Strain. If you want warm tea, reheat it in a clean pan. (Note: Licorice is a powerful herb—it's not just a flavor you taste in licorice candy. Use it sparingly.)

know that you want to remember and work with your dreams, it happens without much effort.

Another vital factor is to respect your dreams and value them. If you think a dream is too silly or bizarre to bother remembering and writing down, you're likely to have more difficulty recalling future dreams. But if you put a positive spin on your attitude, and you're genuinely sincere about it, you'll succeed.

Tips for the Unconvinced

Even if you are not fully determined and convinced that your dreams are worth your attention, but you still want to investigate, here are some tips you can use:

1. Don't eat a heavy meal just before going to bed. Though a full stomach may make you sleepy, what happens is that all your blood goes to the job of food digestion, leaving the brain less blood flow. A lot of food can keep you from getting a sound sleep, so put a couple of hours between dinner or evening snacks and bedtime. Also, don't drink anything containing caffeine—that includes regular tea—and avoid anything really spicy. Herb teas, especially chamomile, are relaxing, as is a cup of warm milk with a teaspoon of honey (the calcium in the milk relaxes the body and mind).

2. Develop a simple bedtime ritual during which you concentrate on the wish to remember your dreams and which will put you in the right frame of mind for your dream self to become active. You might take a short walk, or do a few stretching exercises, or meditate for a few minutes. You can also use the Sequential Relaxation Technique given in chapter 4 or the Mind-Calming Visualization offered later on in the chapter. Or try a relaxing cup of Easy-Sleep Tea (see sidebar for recipe).

3. While you are preparing for bed—washing, brushing your teeth, undressing, saying your prayers—say (to yourself

or to any spirit helper you call on), "I want to remember the dreams I have tonight when I wake up."

4. Practice setting your internal alarm clock to go off fifteen minutes before you usually get up. Do this by telling yourself that you will wake up naturally at the time you choose, just before going to sleep while your mind and body are fully relaxed. This isn't really difficult, because you can program your unconscious mind with a suggestion quite easily when you are in a relaxed state. (You won't miss the sleep because you'll wake up relaxed—not jarred out of your dreams by the jangle of an alarm bell or someone shouting at you to get up and get ready for school.)

5. You can even program yourself to wake naturally during the night after a dream has occurred. When you do, keep your eyes closed and stay in the dream world while you think about your dream. Make brief notes, and then go right back to sleep.

More about Herbs and Sleep

- **Chamomile** is a mild sedative and a sleep aid; it aids digestion, which promotes sound sleep. The tea is soothing, but the extract is stronger.

- **Hops** is traditional for its sedative action. In Europe, hops is often used for anxiety, which is a major cause of insomnia. Use 1/2 teaspoon extract daily. Use hops only at night and don't use it if you're depressed.

- **Lemon balm** is great for relaxing and is best used as an extract, not tea.

- **Passionflower**, or *passe-fleur*, means "flower that excels," but it got its common name from "paschal flower" because it blooms at Eastertime. It is a time-tested remedy for insomnia and anxiety. However, *never combine it with antidepressants or prescription sleeping pills.* Use no more than 1/2 teaspoon extract per day.

- **Skullcap** is an antispasmodic, relaxing muscles in pain or tense from stress.

Teen Dream Tip

If you suffer from insomnia, in addition to hops and chamomile you can use catnip, lady's slipper, skullcap, and valerian root (but do not combine valerian with any prescription medicine used for sleep or as an antidepressant). Steep a teaspoon of any of these herbs—or a combination—in a cup of hot water for ten minutes. Add a bit of honey for sweetening; some herbs are bitter.

Teen Dream Tip
For Girls Only

If you have trouble with PMS or painful menstrual periods, try a tea made from a combination of vervain and lady's mantle. Put one teaspoon of each herb into a teapot and add a cup of boiling water. Steep for ten minutes. Strain and sweeten to taste with honey. Take one cup twice a day from day fourteen of your cycle, or two weeks after your last period started. This relief will allow you to sleep better and get your allotted dreamtime.

Dream Memory Aids

One of the best aids to remembering your dreams is *self-suggestion*. This is a form of self-hypnosis that is very easy to practice. Here's what to do.

1. Be as relaxed as possible before you get into bed to go to sleep. Don't have any input such as TV or loud music before going to bed. Try setting your internal clock, as discussed above, so that you don't need the alarm. If you have to depend on an alarm, set it as low as possible; if you use a clock radio, choose a station with soft, easy music and keep the volume as low as possible so you'll be awakened gently.

2. Once in bed, let your mind drift. Don't pore over the events of the day or go over what you did wrong or any negative experiences you had, and don't get into planning or anticipating tomorrow. Try to turn off your thinking machine. You'll get better and better at this with practice. If you have trouble letting go of your thoughts, try the Mind-Calming Visualization given in the box on page 88.

3. As you drift off into that twilight zone between waking and sleeping, tell yourself that you will remember the most important dream of the night as soon as you wake up. Repeat this suggestion quietly to yourself as you fall asleep. (Be sure you have your pad and pen close by.)

4. Most dreaming occurs in the early morning hours, and dreams that we have just before waking are the easiest to remember. So if you wake up during the night or in the early morning before you have to get up, relax yourself and repeat the suggestion.

5. When you wake up, lie quietly for a few minutes and let yourself remember the dream. Don't force it, just let it happen naturally. Keep yourself relaxed and unhurried for those first few minutes and see what comes into your waking mind. Write down what you remember, even if it's only a word or two, a feeling, an object, or a person.

6. Then, throughout the day, when you have a quiet minute here and there, again tell yourself you will remember your dreams tonight. You can write affirmations too, such as, "Tonight I will remember my dreams." Just jotting these words in your notebook will sink the idea into your memory mind. If you are planning to use a dream for a specific purpose, to solve a problem or get information about something, you can say and write, "Tonight I'll get answers to _____ in my dreams. I'll remember them."

7. Experiment with different ways of enhancing your dream recall until you hit on one that works consistently. Use the suggestions given here or make up your own methods. You can even ask your dream-mind to tell you what is the best way to remember your dreams!

Teen Sleep Needs

A teen needs more sleep than an adult, partly because your body and mind are still growing and developing, but also because your metabolism is different. Research has shown that teens need to sleep not only more hours, but later hours, doing best if allowed to sleep until at least eight or nine o'clock in the morning. Due to school and activity schedules, though, teens don't get this kind of morning sleep, so naps are always a good idea. If unusual sleepiness persists, or if you are chronically fatigued, it may mean that you just aren't getting enough sleep. But there is also the chance that a medical condition needs attention. A dream might even warn you about this. If you are constantly tired or have trouble getting to sleep or staying asleep, have a checkup.

Teen Dream Exercise
Mind-Calming Visualization

Let your mind take you to a beautiful natural setting. It can be a place you love to visit, a place you have seen in a magazine or on TV, or an imaginary place.

You might take a walk through snowy woods, hike up a mountain pass, have a leisurely sit-down by the side of a cool lake, or go to the beach at whatever time of year you like best. The idea is to pick something you find calming and soothing.

For example, try imagining sitting by a lake in spring when the wildflowers are just beginning to bloom. Visualize yourself walking down a country road to the shore of the lake, enjoying the cool yet warm spring air with its breeze that hints of nature's renewal. Allow yourself to feel invigorated yet relaxed. Feel the warmth of the spring sun on your shoulders. You might take off your jacket and turn up your face to its gentle warmth, which foretells the summer to come.

When you reach the lake's shore, find a comfortable spot to sit and relax—enjoy the feel of the grass beneath you, smell the scent of the wildflowers, watch the gentle swell of the lake waters, listen to the birds chirping, see the myriad forms of life all about you exhibiting nature's annual renewal of herself.

Take off your shoes and dabble your feet in the water, feeling its refreshing coolness. Perhaps a small fish nibbles at your bare toes and tickles you. Watch a pair of ducks land on the lake and see the waterbirds soaring overhead in the clear blue sky. Feel at one with the scene. Notice how the water catches the sun's light and see the reflection of a passing cloud on its placid surface.

Take your time to enjoy this place, letting all your worries and tensions slip away until you feel utterly calm.

Once you have done this meditation, you can return here whenever you like. You can change or vary the scene at will. For example, I have a special place I go that is perched on a mountainside. It is the retreat of a Buddhist monk I call Genji. I have been going there for several years, at all seasons, in all weathers, at all times of the day and night. The place changes with the hour, the month, and the season. In winter, I enjoy the mountain's stark beauty, softened by snow at times, and I watch the play of moonlight on the glistening white snow, which enhances the silence. In spring, I thrill at all the little new shoots and buds coming out and eagerly look for the emerging growth. Summer brings things to full bloom and produces brilliant colors in the garden. In autumn, when things are beginning to withdraw into their dormant state, comes the harvest, and the sunsets are of a particularly spectacular beauty. I never tire of this ever-changing place, which always puts me into a state of deep and serene calm.

Teen Dream Tip

Is a Dream Calling You?

If you find yourself sleepy at an odd time—either during the day or early evening—let yourself go to sleep if at all possible. There's a dream calling you! And when these "dream calls" arrive, you'll usually have no trouble remembering the dream. You don't need to "program" anything—there's a message waiting, just like on the answering machine. Be sure to write it down. Even though it might not mean anything at the moment, it will later. These calls from within are important; do not ignore them. Remember that the process of maturing is not one continuous, smooth transition from one stage to the next, like a play or a well-plotted novel, but more of an on-and-off process, uneven at best. We all have multiple selves, and sometimes one of these has got lost in the shuffle of life, bypassed, neglected, repressed. But it's still there, and it may want to speak to you or get your attention through the medium of your dreams. *Never ignore feeling sleepy when you are usually wide awake.* If you absolutely cannot go to sleep (you might be in class or involved in some activity), make a note of your sleepiness and get in a nap as soon as you can. And be on the alert for other episodes of sleepiness at unusual times.

Teen Dream Exercise

Dream Recall

Here is a list of things to ask when you're attempting to recall a dream. Practice on a recent dream, or do this exercise with the next dream you have that you remember.

1. What was the theme or story of the dream?

_____

_____

_____

2. What was the location of the dream: inside, outside, familiar or unfamiliar, the place where you live or somewhere else?

_____

_____

_____

3. What were your reactions to the dream while dreaming?

_____

_____

_____

4. How did you feel when you woke up—happy, sad, disturbed, puzzled, etc.?

_____

_____

_____

5. Was it easy or difficult to recall the dream? Did you remember it as a whole or as a fragment?

_____

_____

_____

6. Who were the people in the dream?

_____

_____

_____

7. Did you interact with any animals in the dream?

_____

_____

_____

8. Was there dialogue between you and others in the dream? What was said?

_____

_____

_____

9. Did the dream affect your waking emotional state?

_____

_____

_____

Bring me all of your dreams,
You dreamers,
Bring me all of your
Heart melodies
That I may wrap them
In a blue cloud-cloth
Away from the too-rough fingers
Of the world.

Langston Hughes,
The Dream Keeper

Teen Dream Activity

Make a Dream Pillow

Dream pillows are lovely objects and very easy to make. You don't even have to sew a stitch! Just get some herbs—hops is best for promoting sleep, mugwort promotes dreams; lavender is a traditional remedy for insomnia, and rosemary is for remembrance; chamomile is relaxing and soothing, while roses calm the senses. You can use any combination of these to make a dream pillow. You can even make more than one, with different herbs, for different purposes.

Get about one ounce of the herbs you have chosen for your dream pillow (dried herbs are light in weight, so an ounce is quite bulky) from a health food store or an herbal mail order supplier. Cut a piece of cloth into two squares about twelve inches on each side. If you can use a sewing machine, or stitch by hand, baste up three sides and then insert the herbs and close the fourth side. If you can't sew or don't have access to a sewing machine, get some iron-on tape; it will do the job just as well. Follow the directions on the package to seal the three sides, put in your herbs, and seal the fourth side. Voila—your personal dream pillow. I make my dream pillows with silk fabric, but cotton is good too. Don't, however, use any synthetic fabric, only cloth that has come from Nature.

You can lay your head right on your dream pillow or tuck it under your regular pillow. Try using a dream pillow one or two nights in a row and see what results you get. You don't need to use it every night, but these herbs made into pillows can't hurt you.

Factors That Affect Dreaming and Dream Recall

There are many factors that may affect your dreaming and your ability to recall dreams—we've mentioned food, assorted stimuli, especially before bedtime, and some other possibilities. The truth is, this is not an exact science, and the only way to find out for yourself is to carry out your own personal research. Your dream diary (next chapter) will be a good place to keep track of your discoveries.

Weather

As with the time of day/night that you sleep, weather is a major, if not understood, factor in sleep patterns and dreaming. How the different weather conditions, and the different seasons, affect each person will be an individual matter. For example, the onset of cool fall weather, especially if it's rainy, seems to induce more dreaming sleep and better recall. Maybe it's because of the comfort of snuggling down into the blankets and being reluctant to get up from the cozy nest of your bed. On the other hand, spring weather—just after winter's frosts—may have the opposite effect, causing light sleep and the urge to wake up early.

The only way to tell which way weather affects you personally is to pay attention to atmospheric conditions and connect them with your dreams and your ability to recall. This is worth a try. You'll probably find a pattern. Weather affects everything else on the planet: bears and other creatures hibernate in winter, trees shed their leaves in the fall, new plants appear in spring, and the summer heat brings fruits and vegetables to ripeness. We humans, being of Earth, are also affected by her seasons and her various weather moods and atmospheric changes.

If you give the matter a bit of thought now, you'll find that you already know quite a bit about your reactions to different weathers. Do you feel invigorated by cold weather, or just want to be a hibernating bear? Does the onset of spring set you singing and dancing

Astrological Weather

From an astrological point of view, our "personal weather" is determined by two things in the horoscope: the *elements* and the *modes*. The elements—**Fire, Earth, Air, Water**—are one indicator of how we will react to weather.

- The Fire signs are **Aries, Leo,** and **Sagittarius**.

- The Earth signs are **Taurus, Virgo,** and **Capricorn.**

- The Air signs are **Gemini, Libra,** and **Aquarius.**

- The Water signs are **Cancer, Scorpio,** and **Pisces.**

How these signs are distributed in your chart will tell what *elemental type* you are. You may already intuitively relate to one of the types.

The modes—**Cardinal, Fixed, Mutable**—relate to the seasons, and the astrological chart will indicate which of your ten Planets is located in what Mode.

- The Cardinal signs are **Aries, Cancer, Libra,** and **Capricorn.**

- The Fixed signs are **Taurus, Leo, Scorpio,** and **Aquarius.**

- The Mutable signs are **Gemini, Virgo, Sagittarius,** and **Pisces.**

For complete information about your personal weather forecast, including exercises for determining your elemental type and for finding your dominant mode, along with detailed explanations of all these types as well as mixed types for both, see my book *Teen Astrology*, pages 59–71. You don't need to know a thing about astrology to use this informative book. An appendix has all the planetary tables you need to look up all ten of your Planets, including your Moon sign, which is coming up next.

or do you feel "spring fever" like an illness and want to mope around indoors? Does bright sunshine with clear skies send you into physical activity, or do you long for clouds and rain? Each person is unique and no one will follow the same patterns. The only way to determine how weather affects you is to pay attention to your own moods, frame of mind, physical and mental energy, and, of course, to your dreams.

The Moon

For the Moon never beams without bringing me dreams
Of the beautiful Annabel Lee
And the stars never rise but I see the bright eyes
Of the beautiful Annabel Lee

EDGAR ALLAN POE

The Moon affects everything on Earth: animals, plants, the ocean's tides, and ourselves. It is, of course, also a major factor in weather and atmospheric conditions, so there's another connection. From an astrological point of view, the Moon's realm is best understood in terms of basic emotional needs, habit patterns, bodily rhythms, and what makes us feel comfortable. The Moon in the sky illuminates what is naturally dark, the night. As shown by the sign the Moon occupied when we were born, inside ourselves the Moon represents our deepest emotional nature, and as such affects how we dream, how often we dream, and maybe how well we can remember our dreams.

For example, a Pisces Moon is the "dreamiest" of all the Moon signs. Edgar Allan Poe, just quoted, had the Moon in the sign of Pisces, as have many other poets who were fascinated with dreams. Poe wrote several poems dealing with dreams: "Dream-land," "Dreams," "A Dream within a Dream." And he often used dreaming as a theme, as in these lines from "Ulalume—A Ballad":

Recommended Reading

You can find out which zodiacal sign the Moon was occupying when you were born by looking at Appendix I, Planetary Tables, page 273 in my book *Teen Astrology*. And you'll find a complete discussion of the Moon in your chart in chapter I, "Why You Are More than Your Sun Sign," on pages 8–9. There's more information too about your emotional nature as it is revealed by your Moon sign in chapter 3, including a full description of the Moon in each of the twelve signs of the zodiac, "Astrotips" for each Moon sign, and how the Moon affects your relationships.

This is nothing but dreaming:
Let us on by this tremulous light!
Let us bathe in this crystalline light!
Its Sibyllic splendor is beaming
With Hope and in beauty to-night;
See! It flickers up the sky through the night!
Ah, we safely may trust to its gleaming,
And be sure it will lead us aright . . .
Since it flickers up to Heaven through the night.

When the Moon shines her gentle light, the doors open to magical realms of the imagination and human creativity, often through the medium of dreams. Usually we dream when the Moon reigns over the world, and from our dreaming comes poetry, literature, art, music, and dance. The Moon represents your feelings—and because the teen years are always full of emotional turmoil and confusion, teens especially can benefit from using the Moon to influence their dreams.

During the hours of night our subtle senses are open and receptive. The Moon symbolizes the unconscious side of human life, and in her dreamy light we can often see more clearly than in the glare of the noonday sun. The sun's light lets us see what is *outside* ourselves—but the Moon gives us a peek into the *inside* of ourselves, which makes it especially important for doing dreamwork.

One of the most important ways in which the Moon affects dreams is through its *phases*. Each month, the Moon goes from total darkness when we can't see her at all, known as the new moon, to the first slender shining crescent, to the half moon, to the full moon, and back the other way again to the dark.

Going from dark to full is known as the *waxing* period, when the Moon increases her light. The waxing Moon brings an energy of expansion, of growth. Under her positive influence, this is the best time to concentrate on new beginnings of any kind, on personal growth, on self-improvement. As whatever is seeded now will eventually grow into fruition, the waxing half of the Moon's cycle is an excellent time

to incubate dreams that will help you grow and develop, to express your creativity, and to improve relationships.

When the Moon is entirely *full*—just before the exact fullness and just after, a period of about two and a half days—the energy moves to complete what was set in motion. At the full moon, the lunar vibes are the most powerful. You can best use this time by saying affirmations before you go to sleep, or by meditating under the light of the Moon before bedtime. As the light of the full moon eliminates shadows on the ground, it also serves to eliminate them within your psyche, bringing clarity of mind and purpose, or emotional balance. The full moon is a good time to ask for dreams that will focus your own energies toward positive specific purposes.

During the second half of her cycle, the Moon is said to be *waning*, or going from full light to eventual dark. At this time, the energy moves toward decreasing and finally eliminating when it is again entirely dark. The waning phase is the best time to deal with any negative issues you want to get rid of, whether this means bad habits, poor health, relationships that aren't working, or any other debris that needs to be removed from your life in order for you to grow and be happy and productive. The waning Moon signals a time to practice releasing and letting go. You can use releasing affirmations just before going to sleep in order to alert your dream helpers of your intentions. Say, "I now release and let go of _____."

The changing energies of the moon work slowly, segueing from one phase into the next in regular, unvarying order. For example, after the night of the dark moon, at the appearance of the first thin sliver of light, the energy of the new moon gradually increases into the expansiveness of the full moon. As the waning phase takes over, the process is reversed as the Moon slowly decreases its visible area and fades away once again. Girls know that their menstrual cycles are related to the twenty-eight-day cycle of the Moon, and sometimes they can time their Moon work to coincide with their periods. Long ago, before artificial light, most women menstruated during the new moon.

Teen Dream Tip

Use these dream affirmations:
- *I trust my dreams to reveal to me my inner reality.*
- *My dreams are gifts for which I give thanks.*
- *My dreams are a form of self-therapy each night.*

But we have not only lost touch with the power of the lunar energies (being fixated as our society is on the sun and masculine character-istics), but the natural rhythms of Nature have been disrupted by our insistence on a "twenty-four/seven" way of life. Paying attention to the Moon's phases and your own inner dream cycles—and female cycles—is an ideal way to reconnect with the never-ending cyclic nature of all that is.

> *The Moon, as the luminous aspect of the night,*
> *belongs to the Goddess; it is her fruit, her*
> *sublimation of light, an expression of her*
> *essential spirit. It appears as a birth—*
> *and indeed as rebirth. Such processes are the*
> *primordial mysteries of the Feminine . . .*
> *from which all life arises and unfolds,*
> *assuming, in its highest transformation,*
> *the form of the spirit.*
>
> ERICH NEUMANN,
> *THE GREAT MOTHER*

6

Keeping a
Dream Diary

*"The Dreamer sees things we can't see and answers
the questions we don't know how to ask."*

RALPH THORPE,
THE DREAMER: A VOYAGE OF SELF-DISCOVERY

A dream diary is a wonderful tool for your nightly dreamwork. Once
you write down your dream—or record it in any other way—you can
"forget" it, because it's captured there in your dream diary forever. Not
only will it help you keep track of your dream patterns, but you'll just
plain enjoy going back over the dreams you've had in the past. Another
advantage is that you can refer to it anywhere along the line—and see
where you've been and what was happening inside you that was revealed
through your dreams. Also, you will be able to understand dreams that
puzzled you at first as you develop a greater sense of your personal symbol system and how it works. So often we have a particularly vivid dream
and remember it quite well and even spend time going over it for a day
or two, but then it fades away like the morning mist disappears when
the sun heats up. When you keep a dream diary, this is no longer a problem. The message of the dream is within your reach permanently.

Perhaps you already keep a diary of your everyday experiences,
thoughts, hopes and wishes, troubles and problems. If so, keeping a
dream diary will be an easy habit to acquire. It's just another type of
diary or journal. If you haven't yet done any journaling, writing down
your dreams is a cool way to start.

The Time Factor

"Reflecting the widespread belief that dreams precipitate from a higher sphere of reality, the study of dreams yields glimpses into the underlying symbolic patterns of daily life before events crystallize into concrete manifestation. . . . The question of how much time must pass between a dream experience and its manifestation in waking reality is often debated. . . . However long this crystallization takes, dreams tend to foreshadow the ensuing physical situation in largely symbolic rather than strictly literal terms. For instance, a dream of falling down the stairs may not herald an actual accident, but rather an emotional fall from grace, such as might accompany a romantic rejection; similarly, a dream of death may symbolize the closing off or transformation of some outworn habit pattern, such as quitting smoking, rather than an actual death."

Ray Grasse,
The Waking Dream

WAYS TO RECORD YOUR DREAMS

There are many ways to record dreams, or bits of dreams, even if only a fragment, a word, a person, an animal. The most obvious way to record your dreams is to write them down—in detail—or jot a few key notes. If writing in the middle of the night or first thing in the morning doesn't work for you, try a tape recorder. You can also draw or paint your dreams or make collages of pictures you have cut from magazines and other sources.

The neat thing about using more than one medium to record your dreams is that it frees you up. Some teens find writing a bore and a chore (too much of that in school already!), but expressing yourself freely in drawing and paint can feel great. Dreams are *always* visual, so using a visual means of recording them only makes sense. And dreams can be very sensual and may have lots of color; I have even seen paintings in my dreams. If you do choose to use one or more visual means to record your dreams in your dream diary, let me issue a word of caution. *Don't get caught up in worrying about your artistic talents.* Just do it!

I once had a beautiful dream and found that writing about the wonderful thing I had seen—two bright Moons shining in the sky alongside each other like Siamese twins—just didn't capture the essence of the dream experience. So I got out my paints and a canvas (luckily I had a tube of luminescent white paint in my paint box) and painted what I had seen in the dream. I called it "The Dream of the Two Moons." It's still one of my favorite paintings. A friend liked it so much that I gave it to her.

A more elaborate way of expressing the "feeling" of a dream is to use clay or plasticine to make a shape, form, or figure. You can also dance your dream and keep notes about how that felt and what you learned. Bodily movement can help to jog the memory and connect you more deeply to your dream experience. You might even think of a particular piece of music that recalls the dream to you and note that in your dream diary as well.

Whatever methods you use, in whatever combination, keeping a dream diary will certainly enhance your dream life—and your waking life, too. Following is a sample of how you might design your dream diary. It's only a suggestion to get you started. Feel free to do whatever you want, however you want to in your dream diary, just using the exercise as a starting point. But do this exercise for a full week before you start your own dream diary so that you'll get in the habit. Take off from there as you choose.

> *The secret of this countryside*
> *Is in the dream.*
> *It is dreamed*
> *Only once, in childhood or old age.*
> *The dreamer is granted the hawk's clarity,*
> *The bee's faceted eye, the omniscience*
> *Of the owl. The land, and all its Joy and terror and*
> *grace*
> *Appear, and appear as a whole:*
> *There are no troubling parts.*
>
> JARED CARTER, "MEDITATION,"
> FROM *WORK, FOR THE NIGHT IS COMING*

Rosemary for Remembrance

You can scent the paper you use for your dream diary to evoke a memory of the dream. Essential oils are good for this purpose, as are other scents such as perfume or bath oils. A sprig of an herb rubbed across a page can be a powerful olfactory reminder if, say, you dreamed of being in the woods or a garden. If you use incense, you can rub a bit of it on a page.

Teen Dream Exercise

One Week's Sample Dream Diary

Date and day of week:

_____

Thoughts before sleeping:

_____
_____
_____
_____

Notes on today's events:

_____
_____
_____

Weather and mood:

_____
_____

Dream description:

_____
_____
_____
_____
_____

Feelings about dream when waking:

_____
_____

If a target dream, list hits:

_____
_____

Date and day of week:

_____

Thoughts before sleeping:

_____

_____

_____

_____

Notes on today's events:

_____

_____

_____

Weather and mood:

_____

_____

Dream description:

_____

_____

_____

_____

_____

Feelings about dream when waking:

_____

_____

If a target dream, list hits:

_____

_____

Date and day of week:

_____

Thoughts before sleeping:

_____

_____

_____

_____

Notes on today's events:

_____

_____

_____

Weather and mood:

_____

_____

Dream description:

_____

_____

_____

_____

_____

Feelings about dream when waking:

_____

_____

If a target dream, list hits:

_____

_____

Date and day of week:

_____

Thoughts before sleeping:

_____

_____

_____

_____

Notes on today's events:

_____

_____

_____

Weather and mood:

_____

_____

Dream description:

_____

_____

_____

_____

_____

Feelings about dream when waking:

_____

_____

If a target dream, list hits:

_____

_____

Date and day of week:

_____

Thoughts before sleeping:

_____

_____

_____

_____

Notes on today's events:

_____

_____

_____

Weather and mood:

_____

_____

Dream description:

_____

_____

_____

_____

_____

Feelings about dream when waking:

_____

_____

If a target dream, list hits:

_____

_____

Date and day of week:

_____

Thoughts before sleeping:

_____

_____

_____

_____

Notes on today's events:

_____

_____

_____

Weather and mood:

_____

_____

Dream description:

_____

_____

_____

_____

_____

Feelings about dream when waking:

_____

_____

If a target dream, list hits:

_____

_____

Date and day of week:

_____

Thoughts before sleeping:

_____

_____

_____

_____

Notes on today's events:

_____

_____

_____

_____

Weather and mood:

_____

_____

Dream description:

_____

_____

_____

_____

_____

Feelings about dream when waking:

_____

_____

If a target dream, list hits:

_____

_____

Teen Dream Exercise

One Week's Visual Dream Diary

If you would rather record your dreams visually, feel free to use the spaces below to practice recording visual images for one entire week's worth of dreams. Or perhaps you would like to make a verbal record in the previous exercise and expand upon that with visual images here. Don't feel that your images need to be representational or realistic. Abstract lines and forms can convey a lot of information about the feeling of a dream, and, of course, I would encourage you to make full use of color as well.

Day of the week _____

Day of the week _____

Day of the week _____

Day of the week _____

Day of the week _____

Day of the week _____

Day of the week _____

Teen Dream Exercise

My Dream Diary Experience

Write a short essay summarizing how your week of recording your dreams in a dream diary has affected your dream awareness and ability to interpret your dreams. Did you notice any repeated images? Could you make connections between your waking state just before sleep and the dreams that followed? Write about anything that feels important.

_____

_____

_____

_____

_____

_____

_____

_____

_____

_____

_____

_____

_____

_____

_____

_____

_____

_____

_____

_____

_____

_____

_____

_____

_____

_____

You'll have an awesome resource in your dream diary. In it you can record not only your dreams but your first impressions and any later interpretations that come to you. A dream diary will trigger insight into your dreams, especially those that seem puzzling. Sometimes a dream seems meaningless, but when seen in a larger context of other dreams it reveals its message.

In addition to all the advantages of keep a dream diary already mentioned, there's another benefit: the more you record your dreams, the more you will *remember* them! It seems that the very act of recording, plus your *intention* to record your dreams, activates the memory function. Like peanut butter and jelly or ham and eggs, the two just seem to go together. The technical word for this is *synergistic,* which means that two things work better together than one does alone. It's as if the brain makes the connection and does it for you once it gets the message of what you want from it—rather like automatic memory training.

As you get into the habit of keeping your diary, you can go on and get specific. Here is an exercise to begin recording your target dreams—dreams you have requested for a special purpose.

"When the state of dreaming has dawned,
Do not lie in ignorance like a corpse.
Enter the natural sphere of unwavering attention.
Recognize your dreams and transform illusion into luminosity."
Tibetan Buddhist Prayer

Teen Dream Exercise

Target Dreams

To do this exercise, select three "target" dreams for each night. Decide in advance what you want to dream about. (If you need to, review chapter 4 about using dreams for specific purposes.) Make a list of your target dreams. At night, read the list just before going to sleep. If, after a week, you don't get any "hits," do the exercise for a second week until you start getting hits. Make notes about the weather, presleep activities, your feelings, the day's events.

SUNDAY

Target I: _____ 2: _____ 3: _____

Time I went to sleep: _____ Time I woke up:_____

Notes: _____

_____

_____

_____

Hits:_____

_____

_____

MONDAY

Target I: _____ 2: _____ 3: _____

Time I went to sleep: _____ Time I woke up:_____

Notes: _____

_____

_____

_____

Hits: _____

_____

_____

TUESDAY

Target 1: _____ 2: _____ 3: _____

Time I went to sleep: _____ Time I woke up:_____

Notes: _____

_____

_____

_____

Hits: _____

_____

_____

WEDNESDAY

Target 1: _____ 2: _____ 3: _____

Time I went to sleep: _____ Time I woke up:_____

Notes: _____

_____

_____

_____

Hits: _____

_____

_____

THURSDAY

Target I: _____ 2: _____ 3: _____

Time I went to sleep: _____ Time I woke up: _____

Notes: _____

_____

_____

_____

_____

Hits: _____

_____

_____

FRIDAY

Target I: _____ 2: _____ 3: _____

Time I went to sleep: _____ Time I woke up: _____

Notes: _____

_____

_____

_____

_____

Hits: _____

_____

_____

SATURDAY

Target I: _____ 2: _____ 3: _____

Time I went to sleep: _____ Time I woke up: _____

Notes: _____

_____

_____

_____

Hits: _____

_____

_____

ADVICE FROM A MASTER DREAMER

The spirit guide by the name of Seth that Jane Roberts "channeled" for several years (and many books) talked much about dreams and dreaming. He suggested that people who have a hard time remembering dreams may have a hidden fear of them, or think they will learn what they'd rather not know. Seth advised that we examine our beliefs honestly. That's the key. By examining what you truly believe, you'll find out what is standing in the way of you remembering your dreams. "You must change your ideas about dreaming, alter your concepts about it, before you can begin to explore it. Otherwise, your own waking prejudice will close the door," Seth says.

Your dream diary is an excellent place to examine your hidden beliefs and fears. You don't have to know what to write ahead of time. You just pose the questions, and observe your thoughts as you write them down. Keep writing your thoughts and ideas, and pretty soon you'll understand something new about yourself.

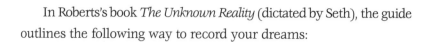

In Roberts's book *The Unknown Reality* (dictated by Seth), the guide outlines the following way to record your dreams:

1. Before falling asleep, imagine you are taking a "dream camera" into your coming dreams.

2. While relaxing totally, suggest to yourself that you will take "dream snapshots" of your dreams while they are happening. "Your dream snapshots will show you the kind of experience you are choosing from inner reality."

3. Don't give up if you don't get instant results. Keep practicing.

4. When you get results, be sure to record *everything* you remember. This is important because the more you record tonight, the more you will remember tomorrow night, and on and on. If you can remember, note how you felt before sleeping and after waking, and how the dream made you feel while you were dreaming and again while you are recalling and recording it.

5. Make notes of atmospheric conditions: Was it raining? cold or hot? a storm brewing? sunny or cloudy? Weather conditions often act as a mirror of the psyche.

Accept whatever you remember, no matter how fragmentary, and never go heavy on yourself for not remembering or for not hitting targets you set the night before. Like learning to play a musical instrument, these things take time. Remind yourself that you are learning a new skill, one that you will have for life and that will only increase as you use it.

A Fragment Is Part of the Whole

In dreamwork, attitude is everything. Valuing your dream product enough to want to remember, to record, to interpret, to commit to finding your own personal patterns—this is what makes everything eventually fit together. Even the tiniest fragment is part of the larger whole—the Big Picture which is your inner self. Trust your dream-self. Interact with your dream-self. Respect your dream-self. You'll receive great rewards if you do.

Dream of the Blue Light

In closing this chapter, I want to share with you a dream fragment I once wrote down, which in time proved to have great meaning to me.

In the dream, I am with a small group of people and suddenly I feel this force. Astounded, I say, "The energy is here," and I see a blue light—like very intense DayGlo or neon—in the shape of a right angle. It is in me and not coming from the outside. I know I am being used as a medium by this force, and I say to the group, "Ask me questions!" They do, and I give answers.

Although I remembered only this slight fragment, it was a powerful sensation. I felt that "the energy" was a real force which had contacted me in the dream state and was using me as a channel for its expression. Upon waking, I faithfully recorded just what I've written above, without a clue as to what it meant. But I *felt* something. Puzzled, I put the written dream in my file of dreams—and forgot about it.

Some time later, I experienced the "opening of the psychic door," and much to my total amazement found I could read minds! Next, I began to channel from sources I could not identify, but I knew they were expressing their knowledge through me. Often, just before something "came through," I'd get a quick flash of bright blue light. Finally, a client said, "What's that blue light over your head?" And then I remembered the dream and understood.

7

Creating Your Own Dream Dictionary

"If one advances confidently in the direction of his dreams and endeavors to live the life which he has imagined, he will meet with a success unexpected in common hours."

HENRY DAVID THOREAU, *WALDEN*

By now you know that the language of dreams is mysterious and powerful. You have learned that you can interpret your dreams symbolically and hook them up to your waking life, influencing it for the better. If you've started to remember your dreams—or even made the decision to try—you are already ahead of the game. Keeping your dream diary faithfully is like having money in the bank. Now let's take the process one step further and talk about how you can enrich all your dream processes by creating your own personal *dream dictionary*.

What exactly *is* a dream dictionary? It's like a regular dictionary: it has words and meanings. The difference is that your words (and images) are symbols that have certain meanings for you alone. A symbol points beyond itself to a deeper meaning. We've touched on the importance of symbols both in dreams and in everyday life. In effect, your dream dictionary is going to be a *dictionary of symbols* that you harvest from your dreams and interpret.

Teen Dream Activity

Create Your Dream Dictionary

A good way to keep your dream dictionary is in a loose-leaf ring binder notebook. Go through the alphabet and mark one or more pages for each letter—more pages for words that begin with the letters most frequently used. For example, "A" would take more pages than "Q" or "Z." The advantage of a ring binder notebook is that you can add pages as you need them. You can also get colored tabs to separate the alphabetical sections. This makes it easy to find them quickly. You might find it convenient to keep your diary *and* your dictionary in different sections of the same notebook.

After you have recorded your dreams in your dream diary, you can go back at your leisure and list the important symbols in your dictionary, along with your interpretation of those symbols. It's a good idea to make notes that refer the symbols to specific dreams and to note symbols that recur. You might use some sort of code—such as an asterisk—to show that a symbol is a repeat. Or you could use numbers to indicate how many times a repeat symbol has appeared. Use erasable pencil for these codes so you can change them as you need to.

UNIVERSAL SYMBOLS

Let's talk about some symbols that usually (but not absolutely always) have universal meaning. These are the symbols that most everyone will interpret the same way, or in a similar way. That's because these are archetypal ideas that reside in the human psyche all over the world. Remember our discussion of archetypes? Here's a refresher:

The person who looks at the world from a symbolist point of view (as do astrologers and some psychologists, mystics and artists, poets and musicians) understands that beneath the complexity of the world that we experience there is another layer that is much simpler than the vast diversity we see every day. There is a primary symbolic language that governs life at its basic, most fundamental level. As Ray Grasse says in his book *The Waking Dream,* "Just as all musical compositions are based on a scale of notes, and all paintings are variations on a spectrum of colors, so philosophers and mystics have taught that all forms or phenomena are reducible to a set of essential universal principles or *archetypes*." Some cultures have identified these archetypes as gods and goddesses, each one representing one facet of the whole of existence.

Archetypes and Myths

An archetype is a symbol—word or image—that arises from a common layer in all human beings, what Dr. Jung called the collective unconscious. While archetypes have universal meaning, they also take on personal coloration and we give them our own individual interpretations, depending on circumstances, the context in which they appear in our dream, and how we relate to the symbol. Archetypes recur in mythology, often as themes. The hero is one such theme and is perfectly expressed by the mythic character of Luke Skywalker.

Whether you consciously recognize an archetype when you encounter one in a dream isn't the most important thing—it will "speak" to you in your own language that you can understand if you try. At some inner level, you'll feel a "click" and just know the meaning of the symbol. It's a feeling or sense of being just right.

Every one of us has ancestors—generations and generations of them—and the fact that we all come from an endless line of forebears creates such archetypes as the Old Man, the Wise Woman, the Mother, the Father, and so on. Sometimes a figure of a woman represents the Goddess archetype, and depending on your beliefs, you may experience other religious symbols. For Christians, the cross is a powerful symbol, while people with different beliefs will dream of religious symbols appropriate to what their culture has taught them.

In astrology, every planet symbolizes something different—the Sun is your core self; the Moon, your emotions and your body; Venus, your love nature; Mars, your essential life energy; Jupiter, the principle of expansion; Saturn, the principle of restriction and limitation; and so on. The Earth is a powerful symbol of home, of growth, of humanity itself and of all the creatures and plants and inorganic forms that the earth has on it. Also, each of the zodiacal signs has a specific symbolic meaning. (See my book *Teen Astrology* for complete information.)

Water is a basic archetypal symbol. It usually represents the unconscious processes, especially if it shows up as the ocean, with its ceaseless movements and crashing waves or its outgoing tide which returns the waters to their central source. As the poet Howard Moss has said, "All the waters of the Earth are one." What happens in the Gulf Stream off the coast of Mexico affects the Indian Ocean on the other side of the earth. The deep ocean currents create the world's weather. It's a mistake to believe that the oceans with their separate names don't have any connection with one another. Every river on earth flows to the sea, and rivers are fed by the snow melt that runs down the mountains. All is connected. This is a prime example of a universal archetype.

However, although water is generally accepted as representing the unconscious at the symbolic level, that doesn't mean that *you* can't

derive a different meaning from water in a dream. Maybe you are planning a fishing trip with your father, or going to spend a vacation at a lakeside cottage with your family, or have had a boating or water-related accident. Water—depending on what form it takes in your dream—may have a purely personal meaning.

But it's good to know that there are universal meanings as well. For example, if you dream you are adrift in a small boat on a large ocean, and there's no personal meaning you can figure out, then it's sure the water is a reference to your unconscious processes. In this example the ocean could indicate you are out of touch with your unconscious. Or, say you choose in the dream to dive off the boat into the unknown deep. Then you would be experiencing the desire to delve into your unconscious sphere of being and learn more about what's there. The feeling you have during and after the dream would reveal your attitude about investigating your unconscious self. If, in the boat that is adrift, you are clinging to the boat and afraid of the water, you might be fearful of being sucked into the unconscious against your will. On the other hand, in the scene where you dive into the water, you are willing to test the unknown depths for the sake of discovering more about your inner self.

When water shows up in one of your dreams, the first thing to do is to note the kind of water it was: ocean, lake, river, stream, a glass of water, a flood—there are many possibilities. Then think of what that kind of water means to you—and see if you can make a connection to the universal symbol of water through the personal symbol. This kind of relating of dream symbols takes a bit of thought, but it's lots of fun—like reading a mystery novel or doing an interesting puzzle.

The important thing about symbols, whether universal or strictly personal, is their ability to connect things—events, persons, feelings, and so forth. As Carl Jung remarks in his book *The Symbolic Life,* "You are standing on the sea-shore and the waves wash up an old hat, an old box, a shoe, a dead fish, and there they lie on the shore. You say: 'Chance; nonsense!' The Chinese mind asks 'What does it mean that these things are together?'"

A Word of Caution

Don't rely on bought "dream dictionaries" that give prefabricated meanings to any and all objects, people, and situations that might occur. If you have such a book, throw it away right now. Not only are these standardized lists wrong, but they can get you off the track of finding out what your own dream symbols mean to you. You don't want to pollute your personal dream dictionary by using somebody else's made-up idea of what a particular symbol means. I've read lots of these so-called dream dictionaries and I find them worse than useless. Sure, they are popular—but they are at best unreliable and at worst misleading. So stay away from prepackaged dream symbol interpretations and make your own personal dream dictionary! That's not only the best way to learn the special language of your dreams, it's the only way. Especially since dream language has more to do with the images and the feelings you have about them than it does with words describing them.

Here's a pretty silly example I found in one of the prefab dictionaries. "Lace means good times ahead. If a man dreams of lace, he will get a job promotion. When a woman dreams of lace, it means a wealthy man will propose to her."

The fact is, lace could mean all sorts of things to different people—shoelaces, or lacing a drink with alcohol, or someone might know a person with the name of Lace. A teen girl might be sewing a dress with lace trimmings for a party. Would her dreaming of lace lead to a marriage proposal from a wealthy man? Not likely. I rather doubt that a teen boy would dream about lace, but let's say he does. Would he get a job promotion? Fat chance, since he probably doesn't work. See what I mean about stupid?

Teen Dream Exercise

Universal Symbols and You

Using what you've learned about basic archetypal symbols, make a list of as many symbols as you can think of that might have universal significance. Then, make notes of what these same symbols mean to you at a personal level.

Symbol:_____

Universal meaning: _____

Personal meaning: _____

Symbol:_____

Universal meaning: _____

Personal meaning: _____

Symbol:_____

Universal meaning: _____

Personal meaning: _____

Symbol:_____

Universal meaning: _____

Personal meaning: _____

Symbol:_____

Universal meaning: _____

Personal meaning: _____

Yourself or Someone Else?

One theory holds that *all* of the people in a dream are facets of ourselves. Personally, I don't agree. Of course, it is entirely possible that unknown persons who appear in our dreams *do* represent parts of ourselves, either that we don't know about or are trying to hide from ourselves. But if you dream of a person you know—or even of someone you don't know, such as a celebrity—there's usually a symbolic meaning to be gleaned from the appearance of that particular person. Say you dream of a character you saw in a movie, or one who appears regularly on a TV sitcom. What would this character, or actor, symbolize to you? Maybe you wish you were more like that character. Maybe he or she represents some quality you need to solve a problem. Or maybe you think he or she is dumb, boring, or unattractive. If you can relate the character/actor to some part of yourself—what you want to be or something you don't like in yourself that you'd like to change—then his/her appearance could represent a side of yourself.

However, that is not necessarily the case at all. For example, I once dreamed of Oprah Winfrey. Though I think she's a nice lady and I admire her success, I've never watched her program. Why would I dream of her? She is certainly not any "part" of myself. Guess what? I received a call from one of her producers asking me about appearing on her show! It didn't pan out, but the dream may have been advance information that the invitation would come.

Let's say you dream about Dorothy in *The Wizard of Oz*. She *might* be a part of you; you might see yourself as the heroine solving her problems. But maybe you've just seen the movie in a TV rerun for the first time and enjoyed it a lot. Maybe you live in Kansas! Maybe you admired Dorothy's spunk in getting herself home and coping with the wicked witch. Maybe you need some of that spunk and your dream is telling you to be more like Dorothy. Maybe you think someone in your life is a wicked witch—a teacher, even your mother (for the moment).

Teen Dream Tips

- Record your dream symbols in different colors—fine-line markers are good for this, or colored pencils—so they will stand out in your dream diary.

- Make a list of symbols that reappear frequently and see if they have different meanings to you at different times in different dreams.

- Dialogue with your dream symbols. Interview *them!* (See the dream interview exercise.) Let them "speak" to you directly.

- Write letters to your dream symbols or figures (animal or human).

"One does not dream, one is dreamed. We undergo the dream; we are the objects."

Carl G. Jung

"The most beautiful thing we can experience is the mysterious. It is the source of all true art and all science. He to whom this emotion is a stranger, who can no longer pause to wonder and stand rapt in awe, is as good as dead: his eyes are closed."

Albert Einstein

Teen Dream Exercise

The Dream Interview

One neat way to get at the meaning of the symbols in your dreams is by conducting a "dream interview" with yourself. In this exercise, you are going to be both the interviewer and the subject of the interview. Think of it as a course in getting to know your hidden self. Here's how to do a dream interview:

1. Decide which dream you will interview yourself about.

2. If you haven't already done so, write out the dream in as much detail as you can and have it in front of you.

3. Before beginning the interview, highlight the words and images that seem to have special meaning, even if you're uncertain about what they mean.

4. Use these highlights as a guide to conduct the interview.

5. Do your interview with a tape recorder, just like a real journalist. Ask questions and then answer them. (Or do it with a friend.)

6. Try to tune in intuitively to the symbols in the dream about which you are interviewing.

7. Ask a question such as, "What does this (describe the scene or symbol on the written-out dream page) suggest to you?" Or ask the *symbol* directly, "Who are you and why did you appear in my dream? Do you have a message for me?" (Later, you can request another dream for clarity if you like.)

8. Answer with whatever pops into mind. Don't sweat it. Take what comes. If nothing comes, move on to the next highlight and the next question.

9. If the question sends you off in a seemingly odd direction, follow where it leads. Symbols are flexible, and one thought about a symbol can lead to a whole string of associations. (Review word associations in chapter 3.)

10. If you (or the other person if you are doing it with a friend) get anxious or uncomfortable, don't push it. Pause and then ask again, gently, what you (or the other) are feeling about the symbol or scene. If it's uncomfortable, just go on to the next highlight.

11. Make a note—verbally on the tape or in writing—of any strong emotions that a symbol or scene evokes in you. Every dream has an emotional heart.

12. Keep the mood lighthearted and playful. Think of this as dream play, not dream work.

13. Do the dream interview like a fun exploration, keeping a sense of curiosity and excitement about what you might find or encounter. Don't get afraid. If something fearful or upsetting comes up, make a note and move on.

14. Have a good time switching roles, if you are self-interviewing. If you have trouble thinking of questions, take the time to write them out beforehand using your highlights.

15. Remember that you can do this dream interview in complete privacy. You can choose to share or not to share with another person.

16. Record all your dream interviews in your dream diary. Then add the symbol definitions to your dream dictionary. And save the tapes.

Teen Dream Tip

You can also do the interview with another person if you want to do "dream sharing," but I know that many teens value their privacy and don't feel comfortable telling their dreams, especially disturbing or puzzling ones, to a friend or family member. However, if you do have someone with whom you regularly share dreams, you can conduct a two-person interview, switching back and forth, one person interviewing the other about his or her dream.

Dream Mysteries

Not all dreams have to be interpreted. A dream interview is fun to do, but sometimes it's better to let a dream just be an interesting experience. A dream can be like taking a trip without a destination. You go where it leads and find what you find. The important thing is to *enjoy* your dreams—even if they aren't ready to be interpreted. Play with your dreams. Toss the images and catch them like a juggler with colored balls. Dance your dreams. Draw them. Catch them in memory's net like beautiful butterflies, just for the pleasure of looking at them again and again. Eventually, meaning will come; and even if it doesn't, you will have had fun with your dream. Sometimes dreams *are* wish fulfillment, as Freud believed, and a rocking good time. And sometimes an unsolved mystery is the most intriguing of all!

Journal Seminars

"In journal seminars, the longest class is always the session about dreams. People bring a collection of recorded dreams, and we set about interpreting, drawing, sometimes acting them out, and nobody wants to go home. It's such a relief to be able to talk about, share, explore this other world in which we spend a third of our lives. It must mean something: we are 'there' nearly as much as we are 'here.'"

Christina Baldwin,
Life's Companion

When creating your own dream dictionary, remember that you—as a teen—are just in the beginning stages of formulating inner symbols and assigning meaning to them. This is an exciting time of your life because you are closer to your unconscious than adults who have many layers of life covering up their connection with their deepest inner selves. It's easier for teens to get at your symbolic meanings because you don't have a lot of learned stuff to shove out of the way of the truth of your inner self.

That's why your own dream dictionary is so important. You will have it to refer to as you get older and experience more and more dreaming and meet different symbols. You'll be able to look back and see what a particular symbol meant to you when you were younger and compare it with what that symbol means for you later on. For example, a teen dreaming about children will have a different meaning than a young mother or mother-to-be dreaming about children. The context of your life will affect the meaning of the symbols you produce in your dreams. If *you* dream about a child, it might be your annoying younger sibling—whereas a pregnant woman would find a dream child pleasant.

Thus, you need to know what various objects and personages mean to *you* so that you will have a clear idea about what significance they have in your dreams. It's fine to tell your dreams to trusted friends or family members who are sympathetic to your dream work, and to get their opinions of what the symbols might mean, but in the final analysis, it's *your* dream and it has to be *your* interpretation. Don't be influenced with what another person thinks your dream means. Make your own decisions. What's key here is how you feel about the symbols—which your dream mind has produced and which are part of you. Also, there's no one way to interpret any symbol. Over time, your symbols may change meaning, or become richer in meaning. There are no right and wrong interpretations. It's all up to you. You are the writer, director, producer, and star of your own dreams. They are your property.

Children's Dreams

The following quotation from *How to Read Signs and Omens in Everyday Life* by Sarvananda Bluestone, Ph.D., demonstrates the importance of the dreams of young people.

> In many cultures the wisdom of the child is respected. In the African country of Togo, children are said to be born with the power to see clearly, and the intuitive clarity of children is recognized as fact. On the other side of the globe, Chippewa Indians of the Great Plains encourage their children to fast and to dream. A child will then be visited by guardian spirits. The adults among the Ute people listen carefully to the dreams of their children.

Teen Dream Tip

To avoid a static outlook on your symbol interpretation, periodically review and update your dream dictionary, noting what symbols appeared in earlier dreams and what you felt about them then. Meanings will change with time. Also, remember that dreams give guidance even when you can't quite get a handle on the meaning of the symbol. Don't feel bad if you have to puzzle over a symbol. That's half the fun of dream interpretation. These brainteasers teach you loads about yourself and how your dream mind functions. And, once you do have a good grasp of what your symbols mean to you, you are in a better position to ask dreams for guidance—and receive the answers you need.

8

Different States of Dreaming

"The notion of this universe, its heavens, hells, and everything within it, as a great dream dreamed by a single being in which all the dream characters are dreaming too, has in India enchanted and shaped the entire civilization."

JOSEPH CAMPBELL, *THE MYTHIC IMAGE*

"There is a dream dreaming us."
A Kalahari Bushman

Are dreams real? That's the teasing question that has been asked for ages. As we have seen, native cultures not only believe dreams are very real, but they use them for any number of purposes, both personal and collective. Our modern society, after centuries of considering dreams to be mere phantoms of the mind and of no importance, began (with the work of Sigmund Freud) to once more pay attention to dreams, but only from the perspective of psychological disturbance. The idea of *healthy* dreams was yet to come.

In the years since Freud we have learned as great deal, through sleep/dream researchers and through individuals writing of their dream experiences. No one would deny that dreams exist; even those who rarely remember their dreams know that they *do* dream, for everyone has remembered at least an occasional dream, or remembers dreams from childhood. The controversy is not whether dreams exist but whether they are useful to our daily lives.

Even the skeptics cannot escape the general fascination that humans feel toward their dreams. Logically, we know (or we think we know!) that we are tucked in bed, secure under our covers in the dark, with perhaps just the moonlight seeping in through the curtains, or even a streetlight's glow. We know that our bodies are not moving. In fact, during periods of REM (when we dream) the body goes into a state of light paralysis and we are literally unable to move a muscle. Yet much is going on. We may be flying, running, conversing, eating, interacting with others—any number of activities that we might or might not engage in during our everyday lives. We find ourselves very active indeed—but at another level than that of the physical body. What's going on?

That's the mystery of dreaming and the fun of exploring your dreams: finding out what is going on and what it means to you. Even if you don't remember what you dreamed, when you wake up you are altered from before you slept and dreamed. You experienced light, color, sound, movements, companionship, animals (who may have talked to you), adventures of all sorts. When you wake up things aren't quite the same. Something has changed inside you. And that inner change slips over the boundary between sleep and waking to affect your daily life, even if only on a very subtle level.

You may find you are in a different mood, either happier or unhappier; you may feel extraordinarily uplifted or have a sense of puzzlement. Wisps of dream may cling to you like cobwebs and you can't seem to brush them off. Whatever happened during your sleep, it is now part of your personal history, just like what happened the day before while you were awake. Perhaps you quarreled with a parent, got a good grade on a school paper, or had a bad hair day. Whatever you experienced during the day has affected how you will proceed on the following day. It is the same with your dreams. What you dream is just as much a part of your life and growth as what you do and feel when awake.

Generally speaking, we have no conscious control over our dreams. Willy-nilly we will dream when we sleep, and there's absolutely nothing we can do to prevent our dreaming, night after

The Chinese sage Chuang-tzu dreamed he was a butterfly, and on waking, wondered whether he then had been a man dreaming, or might not now be a butterfly dreaming it was a man.

"We are in a time so strange that living equals dreaming, and this teaches me that man dreams his life, awake."

Pedro Calderon,
La Vida Es Sueno
(Life Is A Dream)

night. Whenever we settle down to sleep, we spin the wheel of fortune that is our dream life—guided by our unconscious. In no other area of life do we become both subject and object: we are both the dreamer and what is dreamed. But no matter how crowded a dream gets, there's nobody else there inside us. That world is totally our own creation and possession—pretty amazing.

The dream-mind is always telling us stories; sometimes we can make no sense of them but at other times we are illuminated by them and see more clearly, solve problems, get answers. At the very least we are hugely entertained—and sometimes frightened out of our sleep.

In this chapter we are going to talk about the states of dreaming that are different from ordinary run-of-the-mill dreams. Remember the discussion about "big dreams" and "little dreams"? Many of our dreams are just little dreams. Not that they aren't important and valuable; it's that dreams are like much else in life—they vary in effect and intensity. For example, a broken fingernail may be an annoyance to a girl who has just had her nails done before a big date, but it isn't tragic (though she may feel it is for the moment). A broken leg is another thing. See what I mean? It's all a matter of degree.

The different dream topics we are going to cover in this chapter are:

- Out-of-body experiences in the dream state
- Flying in dreams
- Lucid dreaming
- Dreams within dreams
- Dream control
- Telepathic dreams
- Precognitive dreams

- Recurring dreams
- Sexual dreams
- Nightmares and what to do about them

For each of these, an exercise will help you to have the experience in your own dream life and to understand it afterwards. Investigate the potential of your dreams; the rewards are enormous.

OUT-OF-BODY EXPERIENCES

No doubt one of the most interesting, mysterious, and sometimes disconcerting experiences one can have in the dream state is to leave one's own body and go floating around without it! Actually, there's no absolute proof that OBEs (for short) occur *when we are dreaming.* They may be the result of a yet unknown type of altered state of consciousness. However, those who have reported them at least thought they were dreaming, and they knew they had been asleep before the experience.

Though I don't consider myself an authority on the subject, I've had my share of OBEs, each one different (more about that later). But let me tell you about a man who was in the forefront of bringing OBEs to the attention of the public.

Back in 1958, a Virginia businessman and electronics engineer named Robert Monroe had a peculiar experience; to his scientific, rational mind it was a *very* peculiar experience indeed. Monroe had lain down on his couch for a nap and found his body shaking violently, as if his finger were plugged into a live electric socket. He couldn't stop the shaking—in fact, he couldn't move a finger. The terrified man finally managed to get himself sitting up on his couch and then was able to walk about the room. As he did, the vibrations ceased.

Monroe had this same experience repeatedly during the next few months and became convinced there was something seriously wrong

with him, maybe a brain tumor. He consulted his doctor who, after many tests, assured him that his body and brain were in perfect shape. Puzzled but determined to find out what was happening to him, Monroe decided to conduct his own investigation into his weird, ongoing experiences. One night as he lay in bed, he felt the vibrations begin. He had one arm hanging over the side of the bed, and his fingertips grazed the carpet beneath. As the vibrations increased in intensity, he pushed down with his fingers into the rug—and the harder he pushed, the deeper down they went, right through the floor!

Amazed and now more concerned about his health than ever, he again consulted his doctor, who suggested that he might consider learning about yoga. The doctor had heard that yogis could travel in a bodiless state. The notion of such a thing seemed idiotic to the scientific-minded Monroe, who experienced the vibrations another half dozen times before he decided there might be something to his doctor's suggestion. When the vibrations were at a peak one night, he set his mind to floating out of his body—and out he went!

Astonished, and more than curious, Monroe began what was to become his life's work: exploring OBEs. He founded the Monroe Institute, a research and educational institution, and wrote three books about his experiences with OBEs. Today at the Monroe Institute, people are instructed in techniques for out-of-body travel. They learn to follow inner "maps" and see inner "landmarks" and to bring back information from their travels.

An example of leaving the body to gather information from afar is given by Jane Roberts in her book *The Seth Material*. (You'll remember she "channeled" a spirit guide named Seth and produced a number of books that way.) Roberts was of course no stranger to otherworldly matters, and one day she decided to "visit" a couple who were vacationing in Puerto Rico. Lying down, she closed her eyes and concentrated on finding her friends on the tropical island.

Almost at once, Roberts felt herself descending from above, like an airplane heading for a landing. She came to rest on a railed balcony outside a resort motel. She writes, "I knew that my body was in bed, but lost all contact with it. Regardless of where it was, I was someplace else entirely."

Roberts goes on to say how she was memorizing all the details of where she had landed when a noise snapped her back to regular consciousness and she found herself back in her body. Annoyed at being interrupted, she determined to repeat the experience, telling herself she would return to the same place. Her account goes on to say, "Brief but definite traveling sensations followed. Mountains and skies swept by. Then I found myself hovering in the air above the same motel." She kept a record of what she saw, and when her friends returned from their trip they verified every detail.

In the following exercise, you are going to learn the steps for having an OBE. Don't be afraid that this activity can hurt you or that you will be unable to return to your body. *The "part" that travels is always connected to the body by an invisible silver cord.* Remember that this is just an experiment. You may not succeed on the first try, but you can continue trying until you do succeed. Like all else, you are learning a new skill, but one that you already possess within yourself. Many people have OBEs and find them enjoyable and sometimes even useful for getting information, such as when I found out that my late friend had arrived.

More Seth Comments

"In out-of-body states . . . consciousness can travel faster than light—often, in fact, instantaneously. . . . Operating outside the body, consciousness can better perceive the properties of matter. It <u>cannot</u> experience matter, however, in the same fashion as it can when it is physically oriented."

Jane Roberts,
The Unknown Reality

Personal Out-of-Body Experience

The first OBE that I remember took place when I was nineteen, during a nap. Later, unknown "entities" would come and literally pull me from my body, at my feet. I could feel it start and I'd think, "Oh—here I go," and WHOOSH I'd be out and flying around somewhere.

One afternoon a few years ago, I was expecting a friend for a visit at my country house. I knew from past experience that she had a tendency to arrive later than the set time, so I lay down to rest a bit while I waited for her. I was not aware of falling asleep, but I found myself floating around the room and looking down at my body lying on the bed. Still floating, I went to the front door and felt the need to open it for my friend, but I couldn't move the knob. I went back to get my body, but it refused to move. I was totally conscious and couldn't understand why my body wouldn't cooperate. Back and forth I went between the front door and the bedroom trying to get my body to get up. It wouldn't. Finally, I went right through the front door and outside and up the long driveway to the road. There I saw my friend's car turning in. I rushed back to my body and said, "She's here. I've got to open the door. Now GET UP." The next thing I knew I was back in my body, which woke up in the normal way. I went to the front door just in time to greet my friend as she walked up the path. Without question, I had seen her approach while floating free of my body. Apparently my body got in a restful nap while the other "I" was checking to see when my late friend would arrive.

In *The Unknown Reality* Seth says, "In your reality, your consciousness is usually identified with the body . . . that is, you think of your consciousness as being always within your flesh. Yet many individuals have found themselves outside of the body, fully conscious and aware." This is exactly what I experienced.

Teen Dream Exercise
Out-of-Body Dream Experience

There are many ways to have an OBE, but we will use a simple method here to get you started. Then, if you want to explore further, you can. Follow the directions, but expect the unexpected. It's more fun that way!

Step 1.   *Relax.* You can use the relaxation techniques given in chapters 4 and 5 or any others. My books *The Goddess in Every Girl* and *Your Psychic Potential* give some easy relaxation methods. Other books on relaxation techniques are readily available. Explore various methods to see what works best for you. Deep breathing is also helpful.

Step 2.   *Visualize.* As you relax and prepare to drift off to sleep, put a clear picture in your mind of leaving your body. See yourself floating free in space while your body remains in bed. Often, you can see your body there.

Step 3.   *Focus on getting out.* As you drift to sleep, keep your thoughts on leaving your body. Don't try to program how this will happen. Just let the process work on its own. You may feel vibrations or a humming sense in your body just as you are leaving it. This is usual and natural. Don't fear or try to stop. Trust yourself and the process.

Step 4.   *Direct your travel.* To move above in the out-of-body state, you need only think about where you want to go or what you want to do or see. The clearer your self-suggestions are, the better the results. At first, plan only a short trip, maybe just explore your bedroom or part of the house. You can expand your travels as you become practiced and get good results.

Step 5.   *Return to your body.* After you are satisfied with your trip, just say to yourself, "I want to return to my body now," and you will. You might wake up as you re-enter your physical self.

Step 6.   *Record your experience.* If you wake up upon reentry, immediately write down as many details of your adventure as possible. Keep a pad and pen or pencil beside your bed, as instructed in chapter 5.

If you happen to have any negative experience while in the OBE state, or meet anything undesirable, do not become frightened. Simply say, "Go in peace," to any negativity you encounter and continue on your way. If you find yourself feeling afraid, just say to yourself, "Now I will return to my body." Remember that nothing can harm you. Fear is the only enemy, and conquering fear is the way to get rid of it. We'll talk more about that in the section on nightmares.

During times when you are experimenting with OBEs, pay close attention to your ordinary dreams. If you find anxieties or fears coloring your dreams, you will need to discover what is causing them and work through that. It is also better not to try this experiment if you are ill, have been drinking or taking any drug, or are in an unhappy state of mind. Only do this when you are feeling physically well and emotionally content.

Out-of-body states were used by tribal peoples who took group dreaming for granted (see chapter 2). Various tribal members would get together when there was a problem to be considered, such as finding a new hunting ground. All of the dreamers would approach the problem from their own point of view, using individual capabilities, attacking whatever part of the problem each was best suited to solve. Then they would travel out of body in various directions to get information—perhaps about water, food, game, shelter, weather conditions—in order to discover the best thing for the tribe to do. The morning after such a planned group dreaming, the dreamers would confer and tell what they had experienced, seen, discovered, comparing notes to aid them in making the right decision. In a similar manner, tribal dreamers could travel out of body to consult with members of other tribes or villages some distance away to find out what was going on in their neighborhoods and territories.

Today, the TV and radio fill similar purposes, providing a sort of "manufactured dream" to give us the information we need about the weather and what's going on in the world. We have all but forgotten our inner abilities to dream travel. However, there are those today who are practicing what is called *remote viewing*.

Remote viewing is a form of out-of-body travel often undertaken in a trance state (a state of altered consciousness). Some people are talented at doing this, just as some are talented musically, artistically, athletically, and so forth. It is well known that during the time of the Cold War with the Soviet Union, that country was schooling people in remote viewing as a part of its intelligence gathering. It has been said that the U.S. government has also carried on such experiments in remote viewing. Of course, such matters would be kept secret as a matter of national security, but reliable sources have reported that this is happening.

If true (and I believe it is), remote viewing could become a powerful tool not only for gathering military and other intelligence but also for many peaceful uses such as locating lost people and animals, determining the whereabouts of kidnapped children, finding lawbreakers, seeking out contraband, and so on. Of course, we have the Internet for getting all sorts of information about places to relocate, vacation, and visit, as well as for gathering almost limitless information on just about any subject we wish to investigate. Unfortunately, the more we use our high technology to do the job for us, the less we use our own innate capabilities; we are therefore in danger of losing them entirely.

So don't consider your experiments with out-of-body travel to be unimportant. You are keeping alive a human skill that is extremely valuable. And who knows—one day we might need these skills again!

Flying in Dreams

There's really nothing quite so much fun as flying in dreams! It's nothing like flying in an airplane, where the plane is moving but you are either sitting still or walking around just as you would at home. The idea of free flight in space has fascinated humans since time began: sports such as parasailing and jumping from aircraft in free fall are attempts to realize the human dream of actually flying. The urge is so strong that inventors in every century have worked to find a way to fly.

There's a famous Greek myth about an inventor (called *artificer*) named Daedalus who could make and build just about anything you'd like to have. He got in a tight spot where his life was in danger and had to find a way to get over the very high wall that surrounded the kingdom where he lived and worked. So he fashioned for himself a pair of wings made of wax and just soared over the wall to safety.

Unfortunately, his son, Icarus, did not follow his father's instructions (sound familiar?) and, against his dad's advice, he flew too near the sun—and his wax wings melted. End of Icarus.

The famous inventor-artist Leonardo da Vinci was so convinced that humans would one day attain flight that he spent a good deal of his time making models of flying pigeons, and other forms of flight. He filled pages and pages of his copious notebooks with designs of flying machines (actually he was the first aeronautics engineer) and he wrote, "Man shall fly. He shall be as the gods. If it be not for us, it shall be for those who come after us." And he was right, as far as flying machines went.

Everybody knows the story of the Wright brothers, who actually made an airplane and got it into the air, thus beginning our modern era of flight—airplanes, rockets to the moon and beyond, and so forth. But real flying—flying free through empty space—ah, that's another thing entirely. And there's not a one of us who wouldn't give quite a lot to be able to fly (well, maybe a few souls would prefer to keep their feet firmly on the ground). A radio interview I heard a while back gave the results of a poll taken as to whether people would rather have the ability to become invisible or to fly. The vast majority chose flying.

More testimony to our longing to fly is the popularity of the famous comic hero Superman, who can "leap tall buildings in a single bound" and fly around at will. How we would love to be like that fictional creation! And, unfortunately, quite a few young people have made disastrous attempts, from little kids flapping their arms and jumping off barn roofs to teens and college students under the influence of pot or other illegal drugs jumping off balconies, convinced that they could fly.

Maybe you can't fly in "real" life, but you *can* fly in your dreams if you try. Of course, when you fly in a dream you aren't actually flying. (Or are you?) Fortunately, flying dreams are quite common. Many report having them, the exhilaration of them, the fun, the *freedom*. What's more, they are almost never scary; there's no fear of falling.

(There *is* a different sort of dream, of falling downward through space, but these usually come with soft landings.)

Many people stumble over this wonderful ability quite accidentally, as I did. In my first flying dream, I was running down a hill with stones set in it for footsteps and I ran faster, faster, faster until—to my utter amazement—I took off into the air and soared! What a thrill that was. Since then, I always look forward to flying dreams and enjoy them immensely.

Of those who report flying dreams, many do what I did the first time: run, sort of the way a pole-vaulter gets up speed before the leap over the bar. Others say they just flap their arms to become airborne. Some, like birds, simply drift up, up, and away on air currents, while still others say they only have to give themselves the suggestion of flying to experience it with great speed and momentum. Flying dreams vary not only from one person to another, but from one dream to the next, and you can practice different ways of inducing flight. Clearly, there are as many ways to fly in dreams as there are people who dream of flying. However you achieve flying in your dreams, it will be your way—but I'll give you some guidelines to get you started on this fabulous adventure in the exercise that follows.

Dream flying is not only one of the most pleasurable of dream experiences, it can have practical value too. If you fear flying in real life, dream flight can make you unafraid of airplane flying. Dream flying can also serve to release tensions that have built up during waking life—especially those that come from feeling confined or powerless. Dreams of flight are very empowering for teens. They let you revise your ideas of what is possible for you in your everyday life.

According to dream researcher Patricia Garfield, several consecutive dreams of flying are a prelude to lucid dreaming, which we will discuss next. Garfield claims that lucid dreamers (that is, those who know they are dreaming while they are dreaming) tend to have more flying dreams than nonlucid dreamers.

Dream Research

One research study of Japanese and American students showed that about 39 percent of the dreamers studied had dreams of flying or soaring through the air free as a bird.

A team of researchers, R. Griffith, O. Miyagi, and A. Tago, published an article entitled "The Universality of Typical Dreams: Japanese versus American" in the *American Anthropologist* (1958) detailing the results of their study of 250 students in Kentucky and 223 students in Tokyo. In both groups, approximately 39.3 percent reported flying dreams.

Teen Dream Exercise

How to Dream of Flying

Here's how to have a dream of flying. First, as you are going to sleep (and at various times during the day as well), tell yourself you will fly tonight in your dream. Visualize what it might be like and where you'd like to go. Do this in as much detail as you can, imagining the feel of the wind in your hair, how the world would look from high up, what your weightless body might feel like. If at first you don't succeed, keep trying, repeating to yourself frequently your *intention* to fly in your dream. Remember that your intention is the key to success. Try giving yourself a specific goal to accomplish, such as flying down your street, or say, "I want to fly around my house and over the roof." Write out your flying dream intention and put the piece of paper under your pillow. When you wake up, record your experience.

Step 1. Write a definite statement of your intention to fly in your dream.

_____

_____

Step 2. Write a description of what you want to experience while flying.

_____

_____

_____

Step 3. Record your dream in as much detail as you can remember.

_____

_____

_____

_____

_____

_____

_____

_____

_____

_____

_____

Step 4. Give your dream a title.

_____

Step 5. Record the date and the time you slept and woke up.

Date: _____

Sleep time: _____

Wake time: _____

Notes:_____

_____

_____

_____

Tips on Taking Off

Once you have had a flying dream, and you know how you took to the air, you can begin to experiment with other techniques (in your imagination, of course). If you ran and then soared up, try jumping off a rooftop, or stand still and flap your arms, or give a little jump up into the air. Some dreamers report skimming just over the earth's surface like a low-flying insect and then gradually gaining height. You can even jump out of a small airplane and just keep going in the air as long as you like. Whatever works for you! And if you find a way that works consistently, you don't have to find other techniques. You can stick with the one that works. (Others may develop without your even trying.)

LUCID DREAMING

"Dreaming is the bona fide art of breaking the barriers of normal perception."

Carlos Casteneda

Lucid dreaming is the state of knowing you are dreaming while you are dreaming. This may sound like a contradiction in terms, but many people report lucid dreaming, including subjects in sleep research laboratories. Lucid dreaming sometimes happens without your trying to make it happen, but most of the time people who practice lucid dreaming do so deliberately, often for the purpose of controlling the dream, which subject we will discuss later.

Becoming lucid in your dream can take various forms, from a simple realization of "I'm dreaming this" to a complex sensation of being free from everyday restrictions and the realization that, while dreaming, you can do anything you want to do—anything at all. "It's only a dream," you say inwardly, knowing there can be no consequences even if you do things your parents, teachers, or others would have a cow over. This is quite liberating, especially for teens, who are under all sorts of rules and regulations most of the time.

When you dream and enter the lucid state, you have unbeliev-

able freedom of choice and action. Naturally, you don't want to do anything bad or evil, even in a dream, for that might actually influence your daytime life, but you can certainly make what is wrong right—tell off the unfair teacher who gave you a grade less than you deserved for your work, get even with that bully at school who makes your life miserable, smack your annoying little brother, or make love to someone you find attractive.

You can also take trips, visit friends you like, converse with interesting people, ask for ideas for creative projects such as stories and artwork, interview a famous scientist about your science project. The list is really endless, for you are totally in charge. You can travel around the world to places you may never visit in reality, go into the past or into the future and look around. Most important, you have the opportunity to experience positive feelings about yourself that may be lacking at the moment, to see yourself as beautiful, or handsome, or strong and healthy, unafraid, secure, self-assertive, popular. Anything at all. What lucid dreaming is really all about is to use the complete resources you have already stored in your dream mind *by becoming conscious during your dreams.*

Interacting with your dream figures in a positive way allows you to develop new awareness of who you are—and who you can become—which in turn allows you to integrate that new awareness into your everyday life. Eventually you gain a greater sense of your own identity. This is especially important during the teen years when your identity is still forming and there are many areas of insecurity that you need to settle in a positive manner. When you can see yourself in a lucid dream as *the person you want to be,* then you are in a good position to take the steps in waking life to *become* that person.

Maybe you are shy and want to be more forthcoming. Perhaps you feel insecure about your body and how you look to others—especially the opposite sex. Or maybe you have constant quarrels with your parents about what you think or want to do. By seeing yourself resolving

these problems in your lucid dreams, you give yourself the ammunition to solve them in real life. No, it's not an automatic process. You still have to work at it. But like working out at the gym, you develop new "muscles" with which to accomplish your goals of living your life in a smooth and satisfying way. As Patricia Garfield puts it in *Creative Dreaming*, "As you practice competence in lucid dreams, you will increase its probable occurrence in waking life."

Recommended Reading

Creative Dreaming by Patricia Garfield is a rich source of information on lucid dreaming. She states, "*All lucid dreams,* whether consciousness is attained during the dream or never let go of, *are obtained more easily after several hours of sleep.*"

This statement, based on Garfield's personal experience and her research into the experiences of other lucid dreamers, suggests that your best chance of having a lucid dream will be in the early morning hours. If you should awaken in the night, give yourself the suggestion of having a lucid dream before going back to sleep.

Garfield quotes the Dutch psychotherapist Frederik van Eeden, who kept a detailed diary of his lucid dreams for fourteen years, as saying that "without exception all my lucid dreams occurred in the hours between five and eight in the morning. "She says her own experience has been the same, perhaps because it is "easier to assert consciousness when more rested." Using this information as a base, you can time your efforts to achieve the state of lucid dreaming at times when you are free to sleep during those early morning hours, probably on weekends, holidays, and vacations, or even if you are home sick.

Steps toward Having a Lucid Dream

Your *intention* to have a lucid dream is the master key that will unlock the treasure inside your dream world. *Remembering* is the treasure with which you return from your adventure. Dream researcher Stephen LaBerge states that his lucid dreams increased dramatically when he held tight to the intent to have them and to remember them. "Lucid dreaming rarely occurs without our intending it, which means having the mental set to recognize when we are dreaming: thus, intention forms a part of any deliberate effort to induce lucid dreams." In his book *Exploring the World of Lucid Dreaming,* LaBerge sets up four basic steps, as follows. He calls these the MILD (for *mnemonic induction of lucid dreaming*) technique.

Step 1. Prime yourself to recall your dream. Determine at regular periods during the day and just before sleep that you will recall your dream. (Review chapter 5 for dream recall methods and tips.) Pick the last dream of the sleep period, in early morning, as your "target" to remember.

Step 2. Be prepared to record your dream. Have your pad and pen and light nearby. When you wake up during the night, before opening your eyes, lie quietly and recall as many details as possible. No matter how sleepy you are or how much you want to go back to sleep, make yourself write down the dream, even if in shorthand or jotted notes. Don't kid yourself that you'll remember it all in the morning just because it was so vivid. Chances are you won't.

Step 3. Restate your intent as you go back to sleep. This step is vital. When you are in the in-between state of sleep and wakefulness, enough to record the dream, your unconscious mind is most open to suggestion.

Books about Lucid Dreaming

- *Breakthrough Dreaming: How to Tap the Power of Your 24-Hour Mind,* by Gayle Delaney

- *Lucid Dreaming,* by Stephen LaBerge

- *The Lucid Dreamer,* by Malcolm Godwin

- *PsychoNavigation,* by John Perkins

"Was it a vision or a waking dream?"

John Keats

Step 4. Restate what you told yourself during the day and before going to sleep. Visualize having a lucid dream as best you can. (Again, your half-asleep mind will be most receptive to any visualization.) The best way to do this is to see yourself returning to the dream from which you have just awakened and reentering it in a lucid state.

An Alternative Method

In his book *The Lucid Dreamer,* Malcolm Godwin proposes an alternate method for inducing a lucid dream that is based on an Eastern technique called *tratak.* In this method, you stare into a mirror until you begin to see your face changing. To do this, set up a mirror on a table where you can comfortably see it, or set a comfortable chair in front of a mirror on the wall. Light a candle and put it on a non-flammable surface, near enough so that your face is easy to see in the mirror. Turn off any lights.

Now gaze at your face in the mirror intently until you see your image waver and change. Try not to blink (eyedrops will help). As your image moves in front of your eyes state firmly your intention to have and remember a lucid dream that night (or early in the morning). Continue to watch your face changing in the candlelight until you feel sleepy, and then go to bed with the thought clear in your mind that you will have a lucid dream and remember it in detail. Give yourself about half an hour for this exercise. Be sure the candle is completely snuffed out before you go to bed.

A British parapsychologist named Celia Green published a book entitled *Lucid Dreams* in 1968. This book, which contained the most comprehensive overview of the literature available at the time, started the trend toward serious investigation of the phenomenon of lucid dreaming. Before Green's book, there hadn't been much scientific interest in the subject (and England is a country where people take parapsychology much more seriously than in the United States). By the late 1970s, after the publication of Patricia Garfield's *Creative Dreaming* and Ann Faraday's *The Dream Game*, scientists began to take note of what was after all an ancient and honorable pursuit of knowledge.

As long ago as the eighth century, a Tibetan yoga master wrote about methods of learning how to have lucid dreams in a text called *The Yoga of the Dream State*. Then, in the early part of the twentieth century, the Russian philosopher P. D. Ouspensky wondered about remaining conscious while dreaming and asked if it were possible, "that is, to know while dreaming that one is asleep and to think consciously as we think when awake?" His answer was "yes," and he proceeded to investigate the matter, experiment, and finally to write a book about his own lucid dreaming called *A New Model of the Universe*, in which he told some of his lucid dreams. It makes fascinating reading, although teens might find it a tad dense and hard going.

Teen Dream Exercise

How to Have a Lucid Dream

Review the steps laid out in the preceding pages. As you are going to sleep, tell yourself you will become conscious in your dream. Visualize what being lucid in a dream might be like, and what you'd like to accomplish. Do this in as much detail as you can. Repeat frequently your *intention* to become lucid in your dream. Remember that your intention is the key to success. Give yourself a specific goal to accomplish, such as feeling better about yourself. Write it down and put the paper under your pillow. When you wake, record your experience. It might happen the first time you try. If not, keep trying until it does.

Step 1. Write a definite statement of your intention to have a lucid dream.

_____

_____

Step 2. Write a description of what you want to experience while dreaming.

_____

_____

_____

Step 3. Record your dream in as much detail as you can remember.

_____

_____

_____

_____

_____

_____

_____

_____

_____

_____

_____

Step 4. Give your dream a title.

_____

Step 5. Record the date and the time you slept and woke up.

Date: _____

Sleep time: _____

Wake time: _____

Notes: _____

_____

_____

_____

A Fictional Example of a Lucid Dream

My dear friend Ardath Mayhar is the author of many works of fantasy fiction. She finds much of the material for her work in her dreams, as did Robert Louis Stevenson. (Remember the Brownies in chapter 1?) She used the following example in her book *A Road of Stars*, in chapter 3, "Backward Journey." It is based on her own extensive personal experience of lucid dreaming. She has graciously given me permission to reprint it here.

The story is about a world-famous ballerina who has become ill and can no longer dance. She returns to her ancestral home in a remote rural area to finish out her life and has this dream experience:

> She knew that she was dreaming. This had happened many times when she was a child; something she longed to do would become real as she slept. It would seem completely true, and yet some part of her always knew that it was only a dream and would end when she woke again.
>
> It was in that way she came to realize that she must dance. In her dreams she could leap high into the air, revolving as slowly as a bit of fluff riding an air current, to descend at her leisure.
>
> She could, in the dream state, attain total control and complete absorption. It soon became necessary that she learn to do that in her waking life, as well. . . . She sank again into dream, this time dancing, moving to Mozart and feeling the stretch of muscles, the tensions and releases, the brief suspension in space as she leaped into a *grande jeté*.
>
> Multiple layerings of her skirt drifted about her legs, and she knew the familiar pain of the toe-shoes, as well as the pressure of the ribbons about her ankles. The music rose in volume, carrying her back through the years, into a time when her body was young, pliant, and painless. The watchful self that oversaw her sleep understood that this could not last. . . . But she ignored it, burrowing deeper into her dream. She leaped, high and far—and she was on a country path leading up to a hill and into a wood. Barefoot now, she ran upward, scuffling hot sand between her toes and feeling the talc-fine powder in her nose and throat. . . .
>
> Intoxicated, she stood on tiptoe and whirled like a small tornado, stirring the potpourri of odors about her. Then she ran forward, down the hill, leaping lightly over the worst ruts. . . . She danced around the last bend in the trail. . . . She would run, just once more, through that field. . . .

It is interesting to compare this fictional account with the true-life story of actor Christopher Reeve, told at the end of chapter 4.

Dream Control

Sometimes it seems as though humans feel it is their natural right to control everything that comes their way, and that they are also hell-bent on attaining that total control. But simple observation of the world around us and what science has done will prove that the control we so avidly seek is an illusion. Track the progress of a hurricane if you want just one irrefutable example of the failure of the human ability to control everything.

The desire to control seems, sadly, to be built into the human psyche, or at least into a large portion of the population. We are seldom able to let well enough alone. The notion that humans can or should control everything they can get their minds around has caused a great many serious problems in our world. When scientists invented nuclear devices, it was with the assumption that they could control the power locked in the atom. Then, U.S. leaders believed erroneously that we could somehow control access to that power. Clearly this was a major folly, as we see and hear in the nightly news about the proliferation of such devices, creating ever more danger to the world and its people. Yet it seems there is no stopping this urge to control, which now extends to our very private state of dreaming. For many dream researchers, control of dreams is now a major focus, something highly to be desired.

I wonder about the wisdom of this focus. So often we humans meddle with what we don't understand, thinking we know all there is to know about whatever it is, often with disastrous results. The human mind, not to mention the human body, is still mostly a mystery even to the most gifted and studious of our countless scientists and university researchers who have devoted their lives to understanding these mysteries.

It is my opinion that the dream-mind has its own wisdom, one we simply don't and probably can't understand. My view is that it is important and valuable to let dreams be, to let them lead where they

Your Dream World

It's important to realize that your dream life is continuous, that it has its own internal organization on levels that none of us can understand. From its rich and limitless resources you are able to draw infinite wisdom and much of the energy you use in your daily life. Many dreams are reflections—even if they seem distorted like in a fun-house mirror—of our daily life, while others come from deeper levels that remain a mystery. Being aware and paying attention to dreams is good, but tampering with their structure may be unwise.

want us to go, to allow them to reveal their vast wisdom in their own way. (Not that we can't "program" ourselves to receive answers to questions, for healing, and for problem solving, but that is a different thing.) Dreams are like taking a trip into the unknown without a map or a guide (though, of course, we *receive* guidance in our dreams, often without realizing it). I like the idea of just going to bed and looking forward to the surprise, knowing it will be an entirely new adventure, or that it will throw light on some life issue with which I need help.

The idea of dream control, as it is presented by writers on the matter, is that you can *direct* your dream to do what you want it to do. This is related to both out-of-body experiences and lucid dreaming, but it pushes the dream envelope a bit farther. In a way, it's rather like modern agriculture. Instead of letting food plants grow in the natural way, horticulturists have come up with genetic engineering to alter Nature's products (which have lived and thrived for millions, perhaps billions of years). Europeans have refused to import what they call our "Frankenfood": such weird things as flounder genes inserted into tomatoes to make them thicker skinned (for longer shelf life and easier transportation—but certainly not for better taste!). To anyone who has eaten homegrown, vine-ripened tomatoes, the supermarket variety measures up like a rather juicy bit of cardboard. Pretty, it is true, but hardly tasty. I prefer my tomatoes to taste like tomatoes, and I prefer my dreams to follow their natural wisdom, which is wiser than mine. However, since dream control is so popular, it is necessary to cover the basics for you here so that you can make your own intelligent and informed choice about whether to attempt this use of your dreams.

A Hands-On Technique

A major technique used in the effort to control dreams is that of locating your hands with your conscious mind while you are asleep and dreaming. This method was developed by the nineteenth-century Russian mystic G. I. Gurdjieff, whose powerful personality dominated those around him. Here is the method he describes:

Step 1. Close your eyes and try to locate your hands with you conscious mind. Do this several times during the day while you are awake. When you lie down to go to sleep, again visualize your hands, one at a time. It's important that you don't just have an image of what your hands look like but that you know exactly where they are situated—alongside your body, beside your head, wherever. The idea is to imprint this on your conscious mind so that you take it with you into the sleep/dream state.

Step 2. As you begin to fall asleep, tell yourself that in your dream you will see your hands and that you will become conscious—that is, you will know you are dreaming—while actually sleeping and dreaming. Tell yourself firmly that you will become awake in your dream when you locate your hands.

Step 3. While you are sleeping and dreaming, if you can locate your hands you will know you are dreaming, and this is a signal you are "awake" in the dream.

Step 4. When you reach the stage of seeing your hands and realizing you are in fact dreaming and awake at the same time, *stop the dream right there, freeze the action of the dream, like you'd stop a video.* This is important to gain control over the dream and its direction.

A Writer's Ability to Control Dreams

Ardath Mayhar, the novelist quoted earlier, told me that she has had spontaneous experiences of dream control. While dreaming, she would get an idea for a short story or a book and find that she could direct the plot/action of the dream along the lines she wanted the story to go. This, however, seems to me more a method of working with a dream than deliberately induced dream control.

Many people who have practiced this dream control technique for years have not been able to freeze their dreams (I am one of them). Some people seem to have a built-in resistance to controlling their dreams. This can be based on fear; for me it is a philosophical decision to let my dream-mind work its magic without my interference. If you run into resistance in yourself while attempting dream control, it may mean you just don't want to do it. Respect that inner message.

Step 5. When you have succeeded in stopping the dream, look around you at all the details, just as if you were visiting a new place. Examine your dream environment in detail and keep the details in memory. Remember that it may take months, or even years, to achieve this state of being able to find your hands and freeze the dream action to observe it.

Step 6. Once you have stopped the dream, you should be able to direct it as you wish. This is definitely not easy; it takes practice and more practice. If you are determined to achieve dream control, keep at it. Practice as often as you can. There's a barrier between sleeping and dreaming and being awake, and it's not easy to get through it.

Teen Dream Exercise

My Attempts at Dream Control

Here's a place where you can record your beginning attempts at dream control. If you decide to continue with the experiment, you should add a section in your dream diary just for this practice.

Date _____

Time of sleep _____

Time of waking _____

Result of attempt to see my hands:

_____

_____

Result of attempt to freeze the dream action:

_____

_____

_____

Result of attempt to direct the dream forward:

_____

_____

_____

How I felt about the experiment:

_____

_____

I would or would not like to try again:

_____

DREAMS WITHIN DREAMS

One of the most fascinating of the mysterious and multilayered world of dreams is the phenomonen of dreams within dreams. These are not OBEs, nor are they lucid dreams, although there is always a recognition at some time or another—sometimes only upon waking—that one has had a dream within a dream, or even a dream within a dream within a dream. The key to realizing you are having a dream within a dream seems to be the sense that you "wake up" while you are dreaming.

Although I've had hundreds of these dreams within dreams, I have found very little written about them in my researches. But Patricia Garfield does mention them briefly, calling them *false awakenings,* and she relates them to lucid dreaming. In *Creative Dreaming,* she says:

> A false awakening is a state in which the dreamer seems to look back to be awake when he is actually still dreaming. This state may follow a lucid dream, a nonlucid dream, or sometimes no remembered dream at all. There may be a series of false awakenings. Dreamers may apply extreme measures to prove to themselves whether or not they are dreaming, misjudge the experience as reality, then believe themselves to waken, later finding that this apparent waking state was still another dream. A cycle of dreams within a dream can continue through three or four dreams.

Because in my research I've found so little material on them, I can only tell you about my personal experience with dreams within dreams, which first came as a major surprise. After a few experiences, I became quite enchanted with this amazing ability of the dream-mind, and though I never tried deliberately to induce the experience, it happens often enough and always seems like an unexpected but wonderful gift.

The first time was several years ago. I woke up—or thought I woke

According to the Native American teacher of Carlos Casteneda, don Juan, regarding dream control, "The most astonishing that happens is that . . . they also reach the energy body [which] can transport itself in one instant to the ends of the universe."

Is It Real?

According to Patricia Garfield, "Philosophers who have experienced a series of false awakenings have speculated that what we believe to be life may only be another layer of dream," which is in line with what Indian yogis believe—that all of life is mere illusion, that "real" life is but a waking dream. Many ancient cultures held this belief.

Nonetheless, illusion or not, we live in a world that is real to our senses, and that world is quite different from the one we enter when we sleep and dream. Whatever your beliefs are about the nature of reality, one thing at least is certain: we do sleep and we do dream. And in our physical reality, whatever its nature, we need to breathe air, drink water, eat food, eliminate wastes, exercise our bodies with movement and our minds with learning and work, and do many mundane tasks (like the laundry and the dishes) just to keep physical life going along day by day. This book isn't meant to answer any metaphysical questions like whether it's all an illusion or not, and I'm not a mystic who can look into other worlds or a philosopher who speculates on far-out concepts. But isn't it fascinating to think about (while folding the clothes or running the vacuum cleaner)? As a teenager, you probably speculate quite a bit on the nature of reality. It's "hardwired" into the human mind to be curious about questions that have no answers at the moment.

up—from a dream and got up out of bed (or thought I got out of bed) only to discover that I could not turn on the lights. Try as I might, going from light switch to light switch and lamp to lamp, I couldn't get a light to go on. This seemed quite odd. Another time, I heard the phone ring but when I got up to answer it no one was on the other end. It took quite a few of these odd occurrences for me to realize what was going on.

Sometimes I am trying to wake myself up and just can't. These are not nightmares or scary dreams, just dreams in which I can't wake

up from the dream. Other times I am doing something quite ordinary, like getting up to feed the cats, and I find that the canopener won't work. I always wake up in my own bed in familiar surroundings and nothing scary has caused me to "wake up" in the dream. Occasionally I'll think I hear a knock at the door or someone calling my name, and I will "get up" to find no one there. After all this time I now usually recognize the clues and understand what's happening. Now I know that if I think I am awake but I can't turn on the lights (the most common clue) I am actually dreaming, and so I return to the *other* dream that was interrupted by the dream in which I thought I had awakened. I can go through several layers of dreams within dreams in this manner, rather like being on an elevator and getting off at different floors, looking around at what's there, and then getting back on the elevator and going to yet another floor of dream.

I can't tell you how to make this particular dream state happen, but if Patricia Garfield is correct, it might occur during an attempt to induce lucid dreaming. Or it might just happen spontaneously, now that you're focusing attention on your dreams. The key is to look out for what is out of the ordinary in your usual surroundings, like my inability to turn on a light.

There is another type of dream within a dream, in which the dreamer wakes to a sense of suspense as if someone were in the room, and may feel apprehensive and "get up" to investigate. But this type is rare: Garfield says that her extensive dream record shows only one instance of this. Celia Green mentions this variation, and I've had several of these too.

What does all this prove? That the dream world is wondrous and filled with marvels well worth exploring.

TELEPATHIC DREAMS

A telepathic dream is one in which you are in communication with another person. Although this may seem odd or unusual, it is quite common. Many, many reports have been given about people who contacted others in the dream state, had conversations, received information, were given advice or guidance. Our species is apparently "hardwired" with telepathic abilities; the trouble is that our modern, scientifically oriented mind-set has labeled the idea impossible, even in the presence of mountains of evidence. Once made up, the scientific mind is difficult to change. The door to new ideas is firmly closed, locked, bolted, cemented shut, hermetically sealed. However, we need not let that deter us from our own open-minded exploration of this most interesting level of the vast dream world.

Some people lump telepathy under the general term of *psychic*, which has a flaky connotation to those who are strict literalists. Pity those who deprive themselves of extraordinary experiences because they are convinced that if they can't see, touch, smell, hear, or taste it, it isn't real. And don't let the closed minds of others prevent you from keeping your own mind open and free. Say, as Shakespeare's character says, "There are more things in heaven and earth, Horatio, than are dreamt of in your philosophy."

Psychic experience of whatever kind, whether through dreams or "just knowing," is intensely personal, coming as it does from the symbolic level in the depths of your being. Where telepathy is involved, no two people will ever have identical experiences. You are the only person who can evaluate the information you receive in a telepathic dream. You can read or hear about what others experience, but yours is yours alone.

You can think of your psychic self as a large satellite dish constantly scanning the atmosphere for signals (especially in the dream state when the static of everyday life is muted and not interfering). You can also send signals like a powerful radio transmitter. None of us has both of these capabilities in equal proportion: some are better at sending than receiving, others are good at receiving and not so good at sending. Like other human abilities, from a talent for music or art to an aptitude for science or math, psychic abilities vary widely. But just as anyone can learn to play the piano reasonably well with effort

A well-known physician, Larry Dossey, who has written several books and was once employed by the National Institutes of Health to investigate "alternative healing," states firmly that what we call *mind* is definitely not located in the brain—or anywhere else in the body. Dossey calls this concept *non-local*, meaning that Mind (with a capital M) is actually *everywhere*, which is precisely what makes telepathy possible.

"Avoid the teaching of speculators whose judgments are not confirmed by experience."
    Leonardo da Vinci

and practice, even if not at the concert-stage level, just so everyone can access telepathic abilities and develop them.

Interestingly, there is also a spillover factor. To continue the piano analogy, if you learn to play one instrument you'll find it easier to play another. If you get good at either sending or receiving telepathically, you may find that you can switch from being a good sender to being a good receiver, and vice versa. The better you get at one skill, the better you will become at others.

The Psychic Landscape

The psychic landscape has many vistas, places for you to visit and explore, become acquainted with, learn the environment. It is a vast territory with many highways that are well traveled and clearly marked; there are broad avenues where those who are familiar with them can meet in comfort. It also has small, twisting side streets and obscure back roads known only to those who have ventured far into the psychic world. There are difficult-to-find paths upon which one might stumble by sheerest accident, or to which one may be led by an invisible guide, leading to enchanted gardens. The psychic world may not be for everyone, but for those who wish to venture into their own inner realms and find the extraordinary treasures there, it is a fascinating place. Many have adventured, explored, learned, and written about their experiences, yet there are trails still unblazed and undiscovered realms waiting for those unafraid to seek them out.

Probably the most familiar of the highways and byways of the psychic landscape is that of extrasensory perception, or ESP, which is another name for telepathy. ESP has been used as a generic term, a sort of umbrella under which lie lots of varying experiences and phenomena for which we cannot account by the use of our five physical senses. The chances are that you have already experienced some form of ESP: it is especially active in young people who haven't yet been told it is "nonsense." As a teen you are closely linked to your ESP abilities since you don't have the adult skepticism and jaded disbelief to shuck off; you are naturally closer to your own true self and inner abilities. Even so, you may have been made to feel that your telepathic messages are suspect and not to be trusted, or been told that they are "wrong" or "bad." This is especially true of those raised in conservative religious households.

If this is true, you may have felt a need to hide or be secretive about your ESP experiences; you may have learned not to tell anyone for fear of ridicule or being shamed. If so, please fear no more. You have a right to all of your thoughts and feelings, and if you attempt to quash or repress your natural ability, you will be cutting off a valuable asset. It would be like refusing to learn to read and write—and indeed ESP is a language of its own.

It is my belief that we possess not only a "sixth sense" but other subtle senses—a whole range of them like the gradations in the color spectrum—and that these subtle senses account for our ESP abilities. This theory goes a long way toward demystifying them and allowing us to accept that we all possess these extra or subtle senses, and that we are entitled to use them to our personal advantage and that of others. So, don't be shy about your own abilities. If you experience a dream that seems to be telepathic—to be sending a message—pay attention. Remember, just as reading improves comprehension and communication, stretching your "muscles" in the psychic field leads to acquiring new and advanced skills there.

Your ESP dreams can be telepathic or precognitive. (We'll discuss precognition in the next section.) Although research has shown that most telepathic dreams—communications from mind to mind—usually involve the people closest to you, such as family members, love interests, and close friends, they can also involve people you don't even

know. Telepathic dreams involving strangers or celebrities, other public figures such as politicians, and both private and public events have been reported. These dreams are as diverse as those who dream them.

The most defining characteristic of telepathic dreams seems to be an extraordinary vividness: often they are more colorful than ordinary dreams and carry a strong emotional content. Whereas it can be difficult to remember ordinary dreams for more than a few minutes, telepathic dreams seem to stick to the memory like burrs.

"ESP dreams show us that the psyche is capable of a wide range of psychic dynamics."

Stase Michaels,
The Bedside Guide to Dreams

Family Telepathic Dreams

Psychiatrist Berthold Schwartz, in his book *Parent-Child Telepathy*, reports that he recorded over five hundred telepathic dreams had by his family members about each other. According to Schwartz, many of the dreams were simple incidents about family life, nothing extraordinary, but the sheer number of examples led Schwartz to speculate that telepathy is the "missing link" between parents and their children.

Some of the most often reported telepathic dreams within families are when one dreams the other is ill, or has died, or is getting a divorce, or undergoing some other life change that was unknown to the dreamer. Upon checking, the dreams were validated. Research with twins has shown that they can even dream each other's thoughts and on occasion have had identical dreams. Clearly there is a lot we don't know about telepathic dreaming that is well worth exploring.

Whether telepathic dreams can be deliberately induced is unknown. Quite possibly the experienced telepathic dreamer can "ask" a dream for information about, or communication with, a certain person and get positive results. For the beginner, however, telepathic dreams will probably just happen. That does not mean you can't make an attempt

Dream Telepathy with a Stranger

In this unusual example, reported by ESP researcher Alan Vaughan, he had a dream two nights after seeing a TV talk show on which one of his favorite authors, Kurt Vonnegut, Jr., was interviewed. Vaughan recorded his dream on March 13, 1970. In the dream, he and Vonnegut were together with several children. The writer was planning a trip and told Vaughan he was going to an island named Jerome.

Curious about dreaming about a total stranger, even one he admired, and being an ESP researcher, Vaughan wrote Vonnegut and told him of his dream. He received a reply in which the writer said, "Not bad. On the night of your dream, I had dinner with Jerome B. [a friend], and we talked about a trip I made three days later to an island named England."

Alan Vaughan's example is astonishing, but not unheard of. I've had and heard of other telepathic dreams regarding people never met—often public figures. Considering the climate of celebrity worship in our culture, it would not be surprising if teens were able to tune in to their favorite celebrities and get a glimpse of what's going on in their lives. However fun that might be, it's not really the best use of your telepathic energies. I think the telepathic dreams we have about our own families are probably of more importance regarding the daily lives of teens.

to have telepathic dreams by using some of the methods already described for incubating dreams. If you want to experiment, choose a family member or a close friend and tell yourself before going to sleep that you are going to have a communication with that person. Don't attempt to preprogram what the communication will be about—just intend to make contact. Remember, intention is always the key to getting the dream you want. You can visualize the person or think strongly about him or her during the day and before going to sleep. Once you've had a success, you will have some clues about how your own personal telepathic system operates and you can go on from there. As usual, practice makes perfect.

Teen Dream Exercise

Telepathic Dreams

Perhaps you have already had some telepathic dreams—think back over your dreams, and if you're already keeping a dream diary, reread it to see if any of your dreams were telepathic. If you haven't yet experienced telepathy in a dream, use the following spaces to record your telepathic dreams of the future.

DREAM 1

Date: _____ Time of sleep: _____ Waking time: _____

Target person for telepathy:

_____

Was telepathic contact made?

_____

Describe the dream:

_____

_____

_____

_____

How the dream was different from other dreams:

_____

_____

DREAM 2

Date: _____ Time of sleep: _____ Waking time: _____

Target person for telepathy:

_____

Was telepathic contact made?

_____

Describe the dream:

_____

_____

_____

_____

How the dream was different from other dreams:

_____

_____

DREAM 3

Date: _____ Time of sleep: _____ Waking time: _____

Target person for telepathy:

_____

Was telepathic contact made?

_____

Describe the dream:

_____

_____

_____

_____

How the dream was different from other dreams:

_____

_____

Precognitive Dreams

Put simply, precognitive dreams are dreams that give us a glimpse of the future. They don't *predict* the future—that can't be done. Let's take a minute to consider precognition in general before we put the focus back on dreams.

Predictions are tricky business, and those who claim to be able to predict the future are usually mistaken, if not fakers. The future is too mysterious for anyone to predict it accurately. Nonetheless, people have always been—and will no doubt always be—eager to predict the future or to have it predicted for them. That's why so many "gypsies" and other fortune-tellers are in business. But predictions are dangerous because they distract us from correctly assessing our real situation and taking the appropriate steps to make what we want out of our lives. Also, predictions of the future have the unfortunate tendency to turn into "self-fulfilling prophecies," which means that because someone *believes* something will happen they make it happen.

One of the many strange and unexplainable facts of history, however, is that some people do make predictions that seem to come true. One of these was a man named Nostradamus, a physician and astrologer who lived from 1503 to 1566. (That was a time when all physicians were astrologers, and astrology was a respected and necessary training for medical practice, not the parlor game and magazine and newspaper column fluff that we see today.)

Nostradamus was without doubt a most unusual man, but there is no way for us to know from this distance in time exactly how he worked. We know he had extraordinary abilities, but how he acquired these is another matter. It is said that he "scryed," or used a bowl of water as a means to focus his mind in order to enter a dreamlike trance in which he saw visions of the future. He correctly predicted the death and the manner of death of King Henry II of France, in a jousting tournament. Writing in verse, he composed and published a book of rhymed prophecies called *Centuries* (1555), which have been studied ever since. Many believe he correctly predicted the appearance of Adolf Hitler, World War II (which Hitler started), the assassination of the president John Kennedy, and many other modern events.

Nostradamus's predictions were not straightforward; his verses (called quatrains because they are written in four lines) are baffling, and more than one interpretation can always be made by the interpreter. One of his many frightening predictions gave a precise date—May 5, 2000—when there was supposed to be a polar shift that would tilt the earth on its axis, causing complete chaos and destruction. Obviously, that prediction at least was wrong. Still, his reputation as a seer was well established in his own lifetime and has not diminished since then. New books interpreting Nostradamus's prophecies are published regularly.

In our own time, Edgar Cayce, known as "the sleeping prophet," made a number of prophecies, some also predicting massive geological changes. According to Cayce, the western part of North America would break apart and California would float out to sea and become an island, or perhaps sink beneath the ocean. The state of Florida would separate into a series of islands. And, "the greater portion of Japan must go into the sea."

Most serious people who study metaphysics and philosophy believe that the future is always in the process of becoming, that it isn't fixed and that it therefore can be altered. This idea is related to the idea that the future of our planet is somehow connected with the consciousness of human beings and that bad things that have been predicted can be avoided if humans will take responsibility for their actions—and their thoughts. Clearly, we cannot achieve change on a global scale without every individual playing his or her part, and according to Seth, who (through Jane Roberts) wrote extensively on this subject, much of this necessary change will take place in the dream states of human beings.

Dreams and Astrology

While space does not permit an explanation of the astrological factors that can influence individuals, you can learn all about this from my astrology book for teens, *Teen Astrology*. Dreams and astrology are quite intimately connected, and if you are serious about using your dreams fully, then knowledge of your astrological horoscope will be of immense help. Another book of mine, *Tarot for Teens*, can also give you valuable information about dreams and dream symbols. In it you will find ways to incubate dreams as well as much more information on symbol interpretation.

This may seem rather complicated, but as teens you are inheriting quite a mess from past generations, and most of you are well aware of the problems facing you in the future—ecological problems, social unrest, wars, nuclear proliferation, and other threats as yet unknown. Your inheritance also includes a vast richness of choice and opportunity to do good, perhaps to join with others who are working on solving one of these problems, as your life's mission. For this reason, paying attention to your dreams for any that may be precognitive is good training for your future, as well as practical for you now in your everyday life.

In a very real sense, precognitive dreams provide you with an important link to your future possibilities. Take them as *symbolic guides*, not as absolutes, and use them wisely, knowing that your future is really up to you. Remember that no one can know for sure what the future holds, but when you are in the dream state your psyche is open to receiving information about your possible future, which gives you the knowledge to act on, to use as *information*. As you become more aware of the possibility of precognitive and telepathic dreams, they will be easier to recognize. Some of you will have more of a tendency to these kinds of dreams than others—and there are many reasons for this, one of which is your astrological makeup.

Here's a brief example of a precognitive dream I had a few years ago while living in New York City. The dream was short: I saw a commercial airliner flying over the sea off Long Island. Next, I saw a ball of flame burst into the aircraft and blow it to smithereens, and I saw the debris plummeting down into the ocean. The dream occurred in the early morning hours, about three A.M. or thereabouts. It woke me and I puzzled over what it might mean. I wasn't planning any air trips; I had not seen or heard anything about airplanes on TV the night before. Yet the dream was so vivid that it disturbed me greatly. Finally, still baffled, I went back to sleep.

The next day I learned that a jet aircraft had been blown up just off the shore of Long Island. The accident was all over the news, and though a huge investigation followed, the true cause of the explosion was (so far as I know) never discovered. Why I would have such a precognitive dream, when it had nothing to do with me on a personal level, remains an enigma. But it did happen.

A totally different precognitive dream came to me while I was in Germany at a health clinic. I called it "The Dream of the Jeweled Serpent." Here I remind you that serpents are symbolically related to wholeness and healing. Prior to this dream, I had spent several years working on an important project and when it was over I was exhausted and unsure of the direction my work would take next.

In this dream, I am given an enormous, beautiful, green serpent, the size of a python. Its intensely colored iridescent body was set with sparkling gems— red rubies, green emeralds, blue sapphires, purple amethysts, wine-colored garnets, lime-colored peridots—and brilliant diamonds. It was truly a magnificent creature. Its glorious eyes were strikingly clear and luminous, like a cat's. As I am admiring my new "pet," it suddenly begins to thrash around wildly, spewing excrement. Shocked and not knowing what to do nor what is wrong, I telephone a friend who is an expert. I describe the snake's alarming behavior and she tells me that when serpents are upset they "shit all over the place." She then goes on to tell me that my serpent is upset because I do not understand it.

As I knew that the serpent does not appear as a symbol in a dream unless a psychic factor is involved, it became clear to me that I had been neglecting that area of my life even though I was somewhat aware, through my studies of symbolism in the Tarot and astrology, that I might be gifted in that area. I began to rethink my life's direction and to get more in tune with my inner self. Only two months

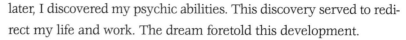

later, I discovered my psychic abilities. This discovery served to redirect my life and work. The dream foretold this development.

Next is an example of a precognitive dream, which foretold my becoming a professional astrologer. At the time I had this dream, I was studying astrology only as part of my interest in symbolism, with no idea of ever reading charts for other people or of "going public" with astrology as a professional endeavor.

The Dream: I am on a train and engage in conversation with a man about astrology. He is very knowledgeable and to my surprise I tell him that I am an "astrologist." He questions me and I give correct answers. Next, we come to the house of a famous astrologer—a sort of palace in the woods. There, I look at a pile of charts and see an error in one of them, which I point out to him. I feel I don't really know enough, but I manage nonetheless. Later on, I find myself lecturing on astrology. The subject is Cancer rising. I answer questions from the audience, and one man says that he has Cancer rising but that he cannot identify with what I have said. I explain to him eloquently that each sign contains within itself its opposite. At one point, still in the dream, I realize that in real life I will one day lecture on astrology, which I have done in real life, as part of being a professional astrologer.

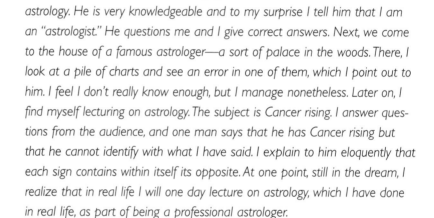

A Precognitive Family Dream

As I was working on this chapter, a friend reported to me a dream that turned out to be precognitive. The dream was brief and didn't have many details. She simply dreamed she talked to her brother on the telephone. What was odd about the dream was that she had not spoken to her brother in years. (Remember about looking for unusual or bizarre elements as keys to these dreams.) There had been a serious family quarrel and the sister and brother had avoided each other ever since. Two days after her dream she received a telephone call from her brother telling her he was clearing out some of the old furniture that had belonged to their parents—actually valuable antiques—-and asking her if one of her children might want to have a dining-room set that had been stored in his attic since their parents died years ago. She was thrilled and immediately called her youngest son, who was most interested in family heirlooms. He gave an emphatic "yes." Then arrangements were made for him to pick it up from his uncle's house. She and I both felt that this dream was precognitive in more ways than one, that the resumption of communication, even at such a practical level, might indicate the beginning of a reconciliation among the family members. A door had been opened and the dream had given her advance notice of this possibility for her future.

Teen Dream Exercise

Precognitive Dreams

Perhaps you have already had dreams that were precognitive. Think back over your dreams, and if you're already keeping a dream diary, reread it to see if any of your dreams were precognitive. If you haven't yet experienced precognition in a dream, use the following spaces to record your precognitive dreams of the future. And remember that research has shown that you don't have to be a prophet to have precognitive dreams: they happen frequently to all kinds of people, from all walks of life. The key is to be *aware* of the possibility.

DREAM 1

Date: _____ Time of sleep: _____ Waking time: _____

Dream description:

_____

_____

_____

_____

How the dream indicated precognition:

_____

_____

_____

_____

_____

How the dream was different from ordinary dreams:

_____

_____

_____

_____

_____

DREAM 2

Date: _____ Time of sleep: _____ Waking time: _____

Dream description:

_____

_____

_____

_____

How the dream indicated precognition:

_____

_____

_____

_____

_____

How the dream was different from ordinary dreams:

_____

_____

_____

_____

_____

RECURRING DREAMS

In chapter 1 you learned about Otto Loewi, who had a recurring dream that gave him the inspiration for his discovery of the chemical nature of nervous impulses, for which he won the Nobel Prize. Loewi had dreamed once of the idea but lost it; then he dreamed it a second time and wrote it down. The rest is history.

Recurring dreams can be extremely important on several levels. Some dreams may be, like Loewi's, of a creative nature, and some are simply your psyche's way of working out its own development. Some can alert us to problems or help solve them, be inspirations, and probably much more. Although in my research I haven't found much written about them, as a psychotherapist I've had many clients with recurring dreams activated by the issues the client was working on in therapy, often relationship or love problems. If a particular symbol, theme, or story comes back to you in your dreams, pay special attention to it: your psyche is trying to tell you something.

At one time I had a long series of house dreams. A house is generally considered a symbol for the self but in my personal symbol system the houses were connected to my father. The dreams themselves were not identical. (Although dreams can recur that are exactly the same dream, over and over, often only a theme is repeated, or a symbol.) However, the general story line of the dreams was always the same: I was attempting to gain possession of a house that I had inherited from my father, and there were always many obstacles in the way.

These dreams were of the psychological type: my dream-mind was working out the emotional deprivation I felt from being neglected and abused by my father during my childhood and teenage years. In a sense, the dreams were taking me through a process to regain what was rightfully mine—in other words, I was inheriting my father's "house," or the love and security I should have received as a youngster but did not.

Some recurring dreams indicate psychological difficulties that need professional help. That is not always true, of course, but it is good to be aware of. If you are troubled about something— either an outside event or an inner turmoil—and your dreams keep reminding you of this by recurring, it is meaningful, especially if the dreams are disturbing. Talk to someone you trust about this. Get some help if you need it, to understand what the dream is saying.

Finally in the dream series, I achieved possession of the house—which was rightfully mine. After that, the dream series ceased.

There are no hard and fast rules that apply to recurring dreams. But there is no question they are important and deserve your attention. Nightmares often recur, and when this happens it can be serious (we'll discuss nightmares a little later). Whenever you have an actual dream recurrence, or if a particular symbol reappears several times or a dream theme is repeated, pay close attention and makes notes in your dream diary. This is one reason that dating your dreams is important. You can spot a pattern. If you make a habit of noting the daily occurrences around your dreams in your dream diary you may find that there is a particular trigger for a recurring dream.

Fear and anxiety can cause recurring dreams, especially in children, and they may be a natural part of puberty (no one knows for sure, as this has not been investigated). If you keep track of your feelings before sleeping and when waking up, you'll get clues about any that recur. Major life changes—moving, changing schools, changing grades, especially from middle school to high school, a divorce, family upsets, quarrels with parents or siblings, disagreements with authority figures (or a run-in with the law), or even contemplating an action you know you should not take—can set off recurring dreams that serve as warnings of a problem you need to handle.

Teen Dream Exercise

Recurring Dreams

In this exercise, you are going to look for recurring dreams, themes, symbols. If you have been keeping a dream diary, consult it for references. It's a good idea to use a code to identify recurring dreams, such as an "R," or to use a different color. Examine any recurrent dreams and put them into general categories such as flying, falling, houses, specific people, travel, and so on. Explore what these symbols mean to you and interpret them accordingly. If you have never had a recurring dream, save this exercise for when you do.

List recurring symbols, themes, or actual dreams:

1._____

2._____

3._____

4._____

Assign them to general categories:

1._____

2._____

3._____

4._____

Your interpretations of the categories and the individual dreams:

1._____

_____

_____

_____

2._____
_____
_____
_____

3._____
_____
_____
_____

4._____
_____
_____
_____

Note what was going on in your daily life during the times of the dreams.
_____
_____
_____
_____
_____
_____
_____
_____

Sex Dreams

Dreams about sex are common, natural, and nothing to worry about. Sex is often on the minds of teens, whether they are sexually active or not. Their bodies are changing and their sex hormones are increasing rapidly. Young teens may still be merely curious about this sex thing; older ones may be reaching the time of beginning to find out for themselves. In any case, because sex is a natural part of human life, as normal as breathing, it makes sense that people, especially teens and young adults, should dream about it.

Sexual dreams are the body's way of releasing sexual tensions that accumulate that you aren't able to physically act on. They can also be helpful teachers, giving you lessons in advance about what sex might feel like. Always record your sex dreams in your dream diary (or keep a separate one if you like, hiding it safely from prying eyes). It's your right to enjoy your own dreams, including sexual ones.

If guilt feelings arise, ask yourself what beliefs, fears, or expectations you have been taught that color your ideas of the rightness of sex. Do you feel that just dreaming about sex is somehow a betrayal of your parents' beliefs? Are you overly concerned about what your parents, your peers, your teachers, or others might think if they knew your dreams? Remember that dreams are not actions in the real-life world. They can't hurt you, and you can't do wrong by having a dream—however steamy—about sex. The main idea is to always take something positive from the experience.

The Senoi people, whom we discussed in chapter 2, believe that dreams of sexual interaction are good and valuable, and they encourage their young people to let the sexual dream progress to fulfillment. Any pleasurable activity in a dream—kissing, petting, fondling—is thought to be a gift; the dreamer is told to continue the dream and to intensify the pleasurable sensations. Wisely believing that one cannot have too much love, the Senoi consider a love dream to be a won-

Sex Dreams and Guilt

Often teens who dream about sexual activity feel guilty, as if their thoughts are wrong. This is especially true of teens who have no real sexual experience yet, and even more true of teens who have been reared in a religion that holds rigid views about sex before marriage being sinful. If you have sexual dreams, please just accept that they are a normal part of growing up. Whether you believe it is okay to engage in sexual activity without being married, or whether you sincerely believe that sex is only for the legally married, *dreaming about sex is not the same as having sex.*

Wet Dreams

It is a well-known fact that boys and men often ejaculate while dreaming, usually just before waking up. These dreams are called wet dreams, for the obvious reason. Girls and women also have dreams that culminate in orgasm.

derful and much desired experience. No guilt involved there! They also believe that the person having an erotic dream should have no inhibitions—that there can be nothing improper about a dream of love and sex because all dream images are simply parts of the dreamer's inner self.

Erotic dreams are most often pleasant, exciting, and fun. You might say they're like eating gooey chocolate cake but without the calories. They're risk free, have no consequences, and are totally private. If you experience them as difficult or painful, examine your feelings about sex and what you have been taught. If you fear sex or have unpleasant sexual dreams, you might want to consult a trusted and unbiased adult for support. There are also several Web sites that offer teens sexual information and advice. (See sidebar.)

Often teens dream about those of the opposite sex (or sometimes the same sex) whom they find attractive. These dreams can come under the category of "wishful thinking," but they also give off information about what sort of person you find appealing. Sometimes sexual dreams make comments about your romantic relationships—a desire to have one, a recent or past breakup, your ideal partner, or what is ongoing in your life. For example, a sexual dream featuring your current boyfriend or girlfriend that doesn't fulfill you might point to hidden problems in the relationship. On the other hand, in a dream about a totally unknown person as a lover, there are clues about what sort of romantic figure you dream about—literally! There's a world of information about yourself to be gleaned from your sexual dreams. You'll find relationship patterns, clues to your most intimate desires (even if unadmitted to yourself), hints about what pleases and excites you, and much more. Don't be shy; don't be afraid. Just dream on.

Remember that just as your body is unlike any other girl's or boy's body, so your sexual nature is yours alone. What is right or appropriate for someone else might be harmful for you, but your sexual dreams can do no harm. They are your *right*. Through them you can learn

The Dance of Romance

To learn a lot about your sexual and love nature, check out *Teen Astrology* (especially chapter 4) by me, M. J. Abadie. This astrology book gives you a wealth of *personal and intimate* information about your unique sexual self. Learning about your Venus and Mars (the love and sex planets) in your chart can be extremely helpful in decoding your dreams about sex and love.

Teen Web Sites

- *Sex, Etc.* @ www.sxetc.org, an online newsletter by teens about sexuality.

- *Teenwire* @ www.teenwire.com, created for teens by Planned Parenthood.

- *All About Sex* @ www.allaboutsex.org promotes positive feelings about sex.

For Girls Only

Research suggests that by increasing sexual expression in the dreams of females, self-esteem in daily life may be enhanced. Patricia Garfield says of this, "If this is so, increasing sexuality in the dreams of a female may have particular value in developing feelings of self-esteem, capability, and other traits of independence. By freeing up our sexuality in dreams . . . we may be freeing creative thinking at all levels of consciousness."

It may work the other way around too. Since girls are more likely to be inhibited about their bodies, which might in turn inhibit their ability to have sexual dreams (or to feel good about them), it's important for them to respect themselves and develop a good body image. To help teen girls do that, I wrote a special book—*The Goddess in Every Girl*—just for that purpose. It's full of self-empowering information about girls and their bodies, emotions, and sexuality. Girl, do yourself a favor, get a copy, and *be a goddess girl.*

"You must honor your body as sacred in order to grow into the spiritual being you are. And to honor your body fully and respectfully, you must become aware of it and what it does on a daily basis. By following the path of awareness, you can reconnect to this inner knowing. Learn to heed the clues your body gives you and follow its directions no matter what anyone else tells you. Regaining communication with your body-self will enhance your sense of living a life that is sacred every day."

M. J. Abadie,
Awaken to Your Spiritual Self

to honor your sexuality as the sacred and precious expression of the life force itself. You will realize that there is a vital connection between sex and spirit. And your dreams can reveal this.

Nudity in Dreams

Dreams of being naked are not uncommon, but they certainly get your attention! Teens may be surprised, shocked, disturbed, or even pleasantly surprised by them. Dreams of nudity may not have a connection with sexual matters in your life. They can point to feeling exposed in some way (maybe in regard to a secret you are afraid will be revealed), or they can be references to something you desire in your life. For example, if you dream of being naked in a public place, it might mean you are longing to throw off your inhibitions about yourself or let people get to know you.

Nude dreams are almost always symbolic, but they can refer to sexual matters too. Author Ann Faraday, in her book *The Dream Game,* tells the dream of a young man who finds himself naked in front of a crowd of his peers who are applauding him. This dreamer had just had his first sexual intercourse and, coming from a background that had made him feel that sex before marriage was not permitted, he interpreted his dream to mean that he had overcome the false and unrealistic prohibitions against sexual activity. Says Faraday, "Had the onlookers in the dream been disapproving, this would have indicated guilt feelings, for in the objective world, his fellow students would certainly have approved."

If you have dreams of being naked, consider the circumstances and emotional tone of your daily life. Ask yourself what being unclothed means to you at a symbolic level. Do you like showing your body, or are you afraid to be seen? Does your body feel like it is yours, or like it is an alien you have to live with? Are you satisfied with it? Are you feeling inhibited or embarrassed about your body or your sexual impulses? Do you have anything to hide or want to conceal (perhaps from your parents)? Are you longing to break through your shyness about being seen as the person you truly are? Have you been taught to think your body is somehow unacceptable (for whatever reason)?

Teen Dream Exercise

Sexual Dreams

Here's an exercise to get you started remembering, recording, and analyzing your sexual dreams. Try not to be inhibited or shy about them. They are for you to enjoy and learn from.

Dream title:

_____

Dream description (be as detailed as possible):

_____

_____

_____

_____

_____

My feelings about the dream (pleasant or unpleasant):

_____

_____

What I learned from this dream:

_____

_____

_____

_____

Dream title:

_____

Dream description (be as detailed as possible):

_____

_____

_____

_____

_____

My feelings about the dream (pleasant or unpleasant):

_____

_____

What I learned from this dream:

_____

_____

_____

Dream title:

_____

Dream description (be as detailed as possible):

_____

_____

_____

_____

_____

My feelings about the dream (pleasant or unpleasant):

_____

_____

What I learned from this dream:

_____

_____

_____

NIGHTMARES

Nightmares—bad dreams or scary dreams—happen to everybody at least once in a while. No one really knows all that much about why we have them, but they can point out problems in real life or in developing into maturity. Sometimes they are brought on by actual events, such as when war veterans have nightmares about their combat experiences.

Children are particularly susceptible to nightmares. Often these can be traced to a specific incident that occurred while the child was awake—a punishment, scolding, or threat of being left alone. Some angry parents tell their children that if they don't do what they are told, the parent will go off and leave them. This is a horrible mistake and a form of child abuse. Of course, any form of child abuse is likely to bring on nightmares. Teens who were mistreated as children may continue to relive those unpleasant experiences through nightmares. If nightmares are recurrent and extremely disturbing, you should seek professional help to solve the problem.

Small children often dream of being chased by wild animals, but by the age of six or seven the nature of nightmares changes and begins to reflect daily life: a child dreams of being abandoned or being bullied by a bigger kid at school. As kids move into their teen years, nightmares tend to reflect inner anxieties and fears as much as or more than actual daily events. The teen years are full of emotional turmoil and rapid body changes.

Adults too have nightmares. According to Stase Michaels in his book *The Bedside Guide to Dreams,* there are three common types of nightmares. In the first type, the person is dealing with fears from real life; in the second type the person is coping with pain and trauma; and in the third, the most common type, the theme can be expressed by the saying, "I have met the enemy, and it is I."

What this means is that the nightmare is showing you a part of yourself that you don't want to see. That part doesn't have to be bad or evil: sometimes we refuse to see what is good about ourselves, especially when our self-esteem is low or our self-image is hurting. And there can be many causes for that. The best way to get at the core problem is to examine your own life, experience, and feelings, and to do this with compassion.

Here are some of the ways to deal with nightmares. First, examine the nightmare to see what you think it means; the significance may be clear without much interpretation. Some therapists who deal with nightmares recommend a method of dream control to cope with them. Another method is to call for help. In a really bad dream, though, you may try to call for help and find your voice is gone. This is when you need your dream friends. Dream friends are figures you have already contacted in other dreams and have interacted with positively. Another method is simply to wake yourself up. Or, if you have practiced lucid dreaming and can do it, tell yourself the nightmare is only a dream and that nothing can hurt you in a dream.

If you are bothered often by nightmares, practice dream control so that you can direct the dream into a positive direction—turn away a threatening figure, make friends with a monster or any scary image, tell what frightens you to go away permanently. (Review the story of Johnny and Dr. Handler at the beginning of chapter 4.)

No matter what the source of your nightmare is (and it may be difficult to determine), it's always a good idea to tell the bad dream to someone you can trust to be sympathetic, ideally a parent. You may need to ask for reassurance if there are any family problems going on, such as an illness or a divorce. Teens are very keen at picking up on anything that's wrong in the family, especially when it isn't being talked about, and such denial can bring on nightmares. If you don't know what's going on, ask. If you have a personal problem that you can't deal with alone, seek out someone to discuss the nightmare with, perhaps your school counselor, someone who is in a position to get you help if you need it. The important thing is to realize that you do not have to suffer alone. However, you can learn to confront your fears and by facing them, conquer them.

Night Terrors

Night terrors are different from nightmares, and they mostly afflict children between the ages of three and eight. However, teens and adults can still suffer from them. Night terrors are horrible images, usually a single one, of being done terrible bodily harm. They are brief but blood-curdling to the sufferer. Psychoanalyst Ernest Hartmann, author of *The Nightmare*, suggests that night terrors may be genetic in origin, running in families. He adds that there often are strong emotions that the person is unwilling or unable to express and that the night terror may be the repression breaking through into consciousness. If you suffer from night terrors, please do not ignore this. There are caring, safe professionals in every city and town who can help you tackle the problem and sort out any issues. If you wait, later on in life they may be harder to dig out.

Dream Catchers

A dream catcher is a circle of wood, usually made from a slender tree branch or a climbing vine like rattan. Inside this wood circle is a webbing that resembles a spider's web. In the center of the web there is a hole, usually with a feather next to it. The dream catcher is hung over the place where your head rests, and its purpose is to "catch" bad dreams and only allow good dreams through the hole in the web. Although this sacred Native American object originally was used to prevent nightmares and let babies sleep peacefully, anyone can use a dream catcher. Shops that sell Native American specialties and many craft shops carry them.

If you want to try making your own, you will find explicit directions in the book *Grandmother's Dreamcatcher* by Becky Ray McCain and illustrated by Stacey Schuett, published by Albert Whitman & Company, 6340 Oakton Street, Morton Grove, Illinois 60053-2723.

Iktomi, the great teacher, appeared as a spider. He taught the people to make webs to catch their dreams so they could reach their goals and make good use of their ideas, dreams, and visions.

Oglala Sioux Legend

Making Dream Friends

In the Senoi system, if a child is frightened in a dream he or she is told to fight back and to call on dream friends. The general rules for making dream friends, as given by Patricia Garfield in *Creative Dreaming*, are based on the Senoi system of dream control. They are:

1. If you encounter friendly dream images or figures, accept help.

2. Express your appreciation for their friendliness and helpfulness.

3. Ask them to give you a gift of some kind—a poem, a song.

4. Share these gifts with others, by dream sharing.

5. Ask friendly dream figures to serve as helpers and guides.

Garfield also says that your daytime activity can change your dreams. "Engage in activities relevant to the dream change you wish to produce; expose yourself to the positive things you wish to dream of; experience the negative things that you dream of in a positive way."

Teen Dream Exercise

Waking Fears

Fears you have in your daily life can affect your dreams, producing nightmares. For example, if you are afraid of snakes, or flying, or water, or public speaking, or taking an exam, or experimenting with sex, or being rejected, or not getting approval, your dreams will reflect the fear. Use this space to list your waking fears and note if they have been mirrored in your dreams. Then think of ways you can overcome your fears in real life.

Things I'm afraid of:

_____

_____

_____

_____

_____

_____

Ways I could overcome these real-life fears; steps I could take while awake:
(List each fear separately and be specific about what you can do about each.)

_____

_____

_____

_____

_____

_____

_____

_____

_____

_____

Make a definite plan for carrying out your self-suggestions and begin at once.

Teen Dream Exercise

Conquering My Fears

Review any nightmares you have had, especially ones that recur or have repeating symbols or images. What do these images mean to you? Where does the dream take place? Are there people or animals that threaten you? Can you relate the nightmare(s) to your daily life circumstances? Are the dreams vivid? Do you remember them for a long time? How do they end?

Describe a recent or recurrent nightmare in as much detail as you can:

_____

_____

_____

_____

_____

What are the most prevalent feelings you have from the nightmare?

_____

_____

Was your reaction to threat or attack the same as or different than in real life?

_____

_____

_____

_____

Rewrite the ending of the dream so that it has a positive outcome.

_____

_____

_____

_____

Dreams about Death

Dreaming of someone's death can be an upsetting experience for anyone, but especially for a teen, because teens are still close to the childhood realm of "magical thinking," where a kind of literalism prevails. However, the vast majority of dreams about death are symbolic of something that needs to "die" by being let go of, such as a relationship that isn't working out or bad habits that are self-destructive. Even positive things can be outgrown: what used to be a healthy dependence can become overdependence on parents, other authority figures, or the opinions and approval of peers. You are now in the process of becoming an adult, and there will be many old behaviors that aren't useful to you as you get older. Often a dream of someone dying is a metaphor for what you need to say goodbye to in your real life.

In *The Bedside Book of Dreams,* Stase Michaels says, "Ninety-nine percent of the time, dreams about death are simply metaphors for major changes happening. . . ." Therefore, if you dream about a death, examine what is going on in your life, your growth and development, current circumstances that involve major changes (such as moving and attending a new school, entering high school or college, becoming sexually active, starting a new relationship or ending an old one, or family changes such as divorce or a parent remarrying).

Though ordinarily, dreams of death are about transformation of some sort, you might possibly have a dream of someone dying while that person (often a grandparent or other older relative) is in the process of dying. Death is, after all, a part of the entire life process—its end: the final transformation. The more sensitive you are in terms of telepathic and precognitive dreaming, the more likely you are to dream accurately of the real death of someone you know—or even someone you don't actually know. Some psychics have dreamed of the deaths of prominent people, and many report that a person recently dead—usually a loved one—has appeared to them in a dream.

9

Dreams and Spiritual Development

Dreams can be a way of reaching the higher states of consciousness of which all humans are capable, if they only open themselves to the possibility. Our dreams seem to reflect our inner spiritual growth and development, although often in rather puzzling ways. You will have a rich variety of dreams that show you how you are growing inwardly only if you believe you are capable of having such dreams. Getting to know yourself better through your dreams is a wonderfully rewarding experience that can be pursued just as you would pursue a friendship or love affair. When dreams "speak" to you, they always have something to say, even if you can't at the moment understand exactly what. If you treat your dreams as valuable and worthy of respect, they'll give you great insight into your inner nature. True self-knowledge in turn can be put to use in your everyday life.

At times of intense growth—and teens are by definition in a process of intense growth all the time—and in times of stress, also common for teens, dream activity may increase or decrease. Usually there is an increase both in dreaming and remembering dreams, especially those from the early morning hours. It's a time to be particularly aware of your dreams, to court them, to dialogue with them. You are being given additional information to which you can respond both with your conscious mind and your unconscious dream process.

Angels

Angels can and do appear in dreams. Look for angels in your dreams, invite them to appear, and they will. I want to share an example of one angel dream that has remained with me in detail for many years now.

As a note to the dream, I should say that I once lived in Italy, on the island of Capri. There I had a close friend, a man named Raphaelle (a form of the name Raphael, which is the name of one of the archangels and of a famous Renaissance painter). Natives of the island of Capri are much closer genetically to their fifteenth-century forebears than are people in other parts of Italy, and the faces you see there could easily have been painted by the great Italian masters. My friend Raphaelle, with such a fifteenth-century face, could easily have been a model for his famous namesake.

Dream of the Angelo

While dreaming of myself as asleep in my own bed, I am awakened abruptly (a dream within a dream) in the middle of the night by a loud knocking at my apartment door, which alarms me because of the late hour. I call out, "Who's there?"

"Angelo!" is the reply, said loudly in a rough, masculine voice with a commanding sound. The voice sounds threatening and I don't know anyone named Angelo, so I remain quiet in my bed. As I lie there wondering what to do, the knocking comes again, louder and insistent as if to say, "Open up or I'll break the door down."

Again, I call out, "What do you want?" but the answer is garbled and I can't understand what is being said. It sounds like some kind of dialect of a foreign language that I don't recognize. Frightened, I remain in bed (still, of course, dreaming) and do not go to the door. I hear footsteps in the hall as the man goes away and I'm relieved.

The dream changes to an evening party that I am giving for a group of

"Whether a holy winged apparition beams silent truths to us in our own room; or a messenger appears in our dreams in the night; or if Heaven speaks through the silences in our soul . . . or the kingdom of paradise within us reverberates with love in our meditations; or our intuition speaks softly in words, feelings and a sense of things to come . . . these are the voices of our angels, gifts that uplift, console, reward, and caress our very being leading us always toward our freedom."

Karen Goldman,
Angel Voices

*friends. Suddenly, I see my Italian friend Raphaelle on the little balcony out-
side my living room window. Sitting cross-legged like an elf, he is smiling, and
as handsome as I remember him in real life. I go to the window to invite him
to come in and join the party, wondering how he got up the three flights
from the street to my window.*

*When he comes inside, he takes my arm and leads me through the
group of partygoers into the outside hall, saying that he has something to tell
me. We sit on the landing together, holding hands, and he begins telling me a
fascinating story about four generations of my ancestors (about whom in real
life I know almost nothing). He tells me that each generation of my ancestors
has written a book about itself but that there is a book left incomplete
because I was not included in it. There is a "missing character," and it is me.
As I listen to the tales of those in my family who preceded me, I am fascinated, and I long to read these books about my ancestors he describes so
vividly. I ask him about the book of my own generation and he replies, "It,
also, is written. Except that it needs you to make it complete."*

*The hall is dimly lit, and beyond the door the party is still going on. I can
hear people talking and laughing, yet I seem to be in another world of long
ago, completely hypnotized by the family story he is relating to me. I feel as if
I had actually known these people (yet even all my grandparents were dead
before I was born). I am wishing I could write such a book as the ones he is
telling me about, but he has said all the books are already written, so I wonder how I fit in as the "missing character." It seems I have to get myself into
the book about my own generation in order for it to be complete—but how
does one get into a book that's already written? I can't figure out an answer,
and he does not give me one.*

*At last he rises to leave, which makes me sad, for I have enjoyed seeing
him again and hearing about the books. I go back inside to find that all of
my friends have gone home, and I go back to bed.*

When I woke up—really woke up—I was so deeply into the dream
that it took me several minutes to realize that I was actually awake
and that I had been dreaming a complex dream within a dream. Sadly,

although I remembered what I have written here, I could not remember anything about the books and what was in them. However, I had the same feeling that I had had in the dream—that I would dearly love to write such a fine book as the ones he had described to me.

After much reflection—for the dream stayed with me—I realized that "Angelo" (angels are messengers of the gods), having been unable to get in through the front door (a symbol for the conscious mind), had become a figure that I could recognize and therefore accept and let in—through a window high off the ground, or into my higher self. His message was clear: I have many ancestors who are unknown to me; however, I am known to them from the "other side." The angel-messenger came to tell me that "I" am missing from the family archives, a way of expressing my "orphan" state of not knowing my relatives or much about them. As my mother died when I was only a year old and as my father was distant from his own family, I grew up mostly alone, without a family.

For many years I had wanted to research both the maternal and paternal sides of my family and to write an autobiographical book about that search and its results. The angel's message to me was that the book was already written—as all books are already written in the divine mind. It was now my job to fill in the blanks, so to speak, to put myself into my own family from which I had been excluded in real life.

This was an extremely important dream for me; it changed the direction of my life and work. It seems that the human psyche is so constructed that the achievement of unity in the internal world causes a similar unity in the external world, like a mirror image: a wholeness between what is inside and outside, which composes a single totality. Only our *thinking* they are separate makes them separate.

Angel Energies

"Right now angels are bridging our physical reality with their pure spiritual energy. Like a leaf falling softly on the still pool of our consciousness, we recognize their presence. As we trust in them, they will pour their blessings on us. . . . And as you become aware of angels [in your dreams] they will be more and more drawn into your life."

Denise Linn,
Sacred Space

"Dreams have always been an important part of my life. I think that is true for most people who are searching for spirituality and go out and fast. Dreams guide you; they show you the way that you should be living, or the direction, or give you signs to help someone else, and they are gifts."

Jackie Yellow Tail,
Crow Woman

"If modern physics is to be believed, the dreams we call waking perceptions have only a very little more resemblance to objective reality than the fantastic dreams of sleep."

Bertrand Russell,
English Mathematician
and Philosopher

GUIDES

A guide, whether in a dream or a vision or in the sense of "just knowing," is actually a symbol for our own deepest wisdom. This inner wisdom connects us to the celestial energies of planets, stars, angels, and whatever else is out there influencing and guiding us without our specific knowledge. It also connects us to animals and plants; to nonorganic life such as rocks, minerals, and all of Earth's materials; and to the cosmos itself in all its vast complexity. Guides are cosmic tour guides—and you can ask for a tour through your dreams anytime you need one by calling upon these spiritual entities. A guide might be an "intelligence" from another dimension, or a stone, or the ocean. The symbols you receive are likely to shift and change over time according to the nature of the subject about which you seek guidance. They will vary also with your state of inner development, your age, your knowledge, your practice, your intention.

We are all capable of contacting the guides of our own deeper dimensions symbolically, especially in our dreams and in altered states of consciousness, which we attain in the "twilight" or hypnogogic time just before sleep, or through meditation. It is through our understanding of our dream symbols that we can connect with what cannot be accessed through our five physical senses—touching, tasting, seeing, hearing, smelling. That's why it's vital to interact with the symbols in your dreams, make the effort to remember and record them, and work with them over time to understand what they mean to you. These dream guides can be very powerful influences in our daily lives, give direction, and aid our growth and development on a spiritual level.

For example, for many years I met with a group of nine old men, wise men or sages, who conversed with me on various topics. In one dream, they gave me a large book made of ancient parchment sheets, yellowed with time but not fragile. Though I could not read the mysterious writing that covered the pages, I nevertheless understood that

on these pages were written important esoteric and magical knowledge. I realized that the nine men were celestial intelligences from the world of nontime, and I called them "the Council of Nine." After meeting them several times, I was inspired to write a poem, "The Return," about my experiences with this group of marvelous dream guides.

Dream of the Great Library

In this extraordinary dream, I am visiting the house of a man who goes by the nickname Winnie (possibly a pun on the word win). He shows me a magnificent library that is a collection of ancient texts on papyrus, handwritten books from antiquity, illuminated manuscripts, medieval books on herbalist lore, mysterious alchemical texts, books of magic spells—esoteric teachings of all kinds and from all ages. It takes my breath away to be in the same room with this knowledge of the ages, written by the wisest of writers. The books are all bound in gold-lettered leather and they seem to glow with power. As I admire the books, he says, "I will teach you all that is in here if you forget about getting your Ph.D." I ask, "What will I accomplish if I learn all of this?" His reply is, "Nothing."

My interpretation of this stunning dream (for I was indeed contemplating getting my Ph.D.) was that I must give up conventional thinking, represented by the academic way of life and by our society's fixation on collecting credentials as the only acceptable path to a successful life. This pursuit of only that knowledge which is taught in our universities would be replaced with the powerful ancient tradition of learning (which some feel is far superior to the dry "book learning" that values only the left-brain, rational mode of thinking and denies anything that cannot be proved in a laboratory).

Seth Speaks

"When you look into yourself, the very effort involved extends the limitations of your consciousness, expands it, and allows the egotistical self to use abilities that it often does not realize it possesses," Seth says in *The Seth Material.* Jane Roberts comments, "According to Seth, these Inner Senses are used by the whole self constantly. Since past, present, and future have no basic reality, this (particular) sense allows us to see through the apparent time barriers. We are seeing things as they really are."

Night Classes

Some fortunate people have the ability to receive "teachings" through their dreams and remember them entirely. Such a person was a woman named Viola Petitt Neal, author of *Through the Curtain*. She reports how she attended "night classes" regularly, the contents of which she dictated to Ms. Shafica Karagulla while she was in the dream state. In their book, the authors speak of a "Council of Seven," who were the teachers. Interestingly, seven is a magical number, combining three (the number of sides of a triangle) with four (the number of directions); it is often diagrammatically shown as a triangle enclosed within a square, symbolizing the unity of the trinity and the four directions (North, South, East, West) on which many cultures have founded their spiritual traditions.

However, my learning the ancient wisdom will not accomplish anything in *this* world, the world of the "bottom line" mentality. That is not the purpose of esoteric or occult knowledge. Although it has certain uses on the mundane plane of practical life, its true purpose is for the development of the spiritual life.

In a similar vein, Jane Roberts told of having had a "vision" of a great library which she could consult at will through her contact with her spirit guide Seth. This library she discovered was full of ancient and all-but-forgotten knowledge and wisdom. Many people who study occult matters believe that there is a spiritual repository of all the world's knowledge, from its very beginnings (which may be much longer ago than our scientists think) and that this repository is available to anyone who seeks to enter it and use it.

POWER DREAMS AND POWER OBJECTS

One of the best ways to contact the spiritual dimension in your dreams is through a *power object*. With a power object, you can obtain a power dream for any purpose you need. A power object can be anything that is important to you, and it doesn't need to have monetary value, although some do, such as a piece of jewelry or other object that has been handed down in your family for generations. I use my mother's wedding ring as a power object. I also use a very special ring that was handmade by a woman who was a well-known psychic and Tarot card reader in New York many years ago. She made the ring for a mutual friend of ours, and he wore it daily for many years. Upon his death in 1999, the ring came to me. Another power object I use is a stone, a "pet rock" that I found on the beach at Montauk Point, New York, while on vacation there many years ago. I have other stones that I've collected from different beaches in different countries over the years, some special shells, and a few other objects I use in dream work.

The idea behind using a power object to obtain a power dream is that such an object has in it a kind of intelligence—stored memories of where it has been and, if it has belonged to a person, of that person and his or her life. Any handmade object will have the imprint of the person who made it. An object you make yourself from materials special to you would be a good power object. And you can have more than one that you use for different, specific power-dream purposes—such as problem-solving, out-of-body travel, precognitive or telepathic dreams, chasing nightmares away, or simply entertainment. Fun and fabulous, our entertainment dreams usually need no interpretation. Flying dreams are extremely pleasurable, as are love and sex dreams. Often entertainment dreams tell us stories of a fantastic nature. (Remember my friend who writes fantasy fiction? She says she gets lots of her ideas from her entertainment dreams.)

In a spiritual sense, power dreams are potent because they connect us to other realities, open our minds to what is possible beyond what we think is possible. If, for example, you dream of a magical crystal or stone, go out and look for one that represents your dream object and use it as a power object.

Dream Cards

Dream Cards, by Stephen Kaplan Williams, is a set of sixty-six Dream Cards and sixty-six Wisdom Cards along with a book explaining how to interpret and learn from your dreams.

Preparing for a Power Dream

Hold your chosen object in your hand while you lie quietly in bed before going to sleep. Quiet your mind by relaxation or meditation. If you know the history of your object, review it in your mind. Allow the power object to grow warm in your hand as you think about it. Be aware of any thoughts or ideas that come to you as you let your mind drift freely. Just before going to sleep, place your object under your pillow or nearby (perhaps on a night table). As you go into the twilight state prior to sleep, ask for a power dream to come to you from the source of the power object. If the object belonged to someone you know (say, a family member) and you remember that person, ask for contact with his or her positive energies. Assure yourself that your dream will be positive and that you will receive the answer to any question, or have the kind of dream you want.

Teen Dream Exercise

Spiritual Life

Write a short essay about your spiritual life, what you believe in and how you feel about those beliefs. Write about what you would like to develop in your spiritual life, what you would like to change, what you would like to experience. Be as detailed as possible. Ask yourself where you are now and where you would like to be in the future. List anything you want spiritual guidance on.

_____

_____

_____

_____

_____

_____

_____

_____

_____

_____

_____

_____

_____

_____

_____

_____

_____

_____

_____

_____

_____

_____

Creating a Dream Circle

A good way to enhance your spiritual development through your dreams is to create a "Dream Circle" of friends who are interested in exploring their dreams and living a spiritual life. To hold a dream circle, choose several friends for an overnight gathering at someone's house. (Be sure to get parental permission for this.) The number should not be more than can sleep there comfortably, nor more than is acceptable to the parents. This is a different kind of slumber party: you are all going to prepare for dreaming and then talk about your dreams in the morning afterward.

You will want this to be a quiet time—no music, TV, videos, or other forms of entertainment. Focus on the dreams to come. Light snacks are fine, but heavy eating may interfere with sound sleep. During the evening, read about dreams together (you can use this book and any others you have on the subject of dreams) and focus your combined energies on your dreams. You might all want to share a past dream that you found interesting, important, puzzling, or otherwise noteworthy.

Make some dream tea for everyone to drink before sleeping, and if you have dream pillows, you can use them too. Ideally, everyone should sleep in the same room. Have an even number of sleepover guests so that you can work in dream pairs. If all cannot sleep in one room, the pairs should sleep in the same room with each other. Arrange the time so that everyone can wake up naturally, without alarm clocks. Make sure your family knows what you are doing so that you won't be disturbed until you wake up.

After waking (some may wake earlier than others) share your dreams with your dream partner (when he or she wakes up), or with another of the dream circle. Talk quietly or go into another room if some are still sleeping. When everyone is awake, sit in a circle and discuss your dreams, allowing time for each person to share her dream without being interrupted. All should make notes for further discussion. Next, breakfast!

BOOKS OF RELATED INTEREST

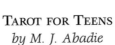

TAROT FOR TEENS
by M. J. Abadie

THE GODDESS IN EVERY GIRL
Develop Your Teen Feminine Power
by M. J. Abadie

TEEN ASTROLOGY
The Ultimate Guide to Making Your Life Your Own
by M. J. Abadie

THE WORLD DREAM BOOK
Use the Wisdom of World Cultures to Uncover Your Dream Power
by Sarvananda Bluestone, Ph.D.

THE THUNDERING YEARS
Rituals and Sacred Wisdom for Teens
by Julie Tallard Johnson

TEEN PSYCHIC
Exploring Your Intuitive Spiritual Powers
by Julie Tallard Johnson

I CHING FOR TEENS
Take Charge of Your Destiny with the Ancient Chinese Oracle
by Julie Tallard Johnson

TEEN FENG SHUI
Design Your Space, Design Your Life
by Susan Levitt

Inner Traditions • Bear & Company
P.O. Box 388
Rochester, VT 05767
1-800-246-8648
www.InnerTraditions.com

Or contact your local bookseller